D1419048

THE APPLICABILITY OF ORGANIZATIONAL SOCIOLOGY

THE APPLICABILITY OF ORGANIZATIONAL SOCIOLOGY

CHRIS ARGYRIS

James Bryant Conant Professor of Education and Organizational Behavior, Graduate Schools of Education and Business Administration, Harvard University

CAMBRIDGE

At the University Press

Published by the Syndics of the Cambridge University Press
Bentley House, 200 Euston Road, London NW1 2DB
American Branch: 32 East 57th Street, New York, N.Y.10022

Library of Congress Catalogue Card Number: 76-185568

ISBN: 0 521 08448 2

Printed in the United States of America
Typeset by Western Printing Services Ltd, Bristol, England

First published 1972
Reprinted 1974

CONTENTS

ACKNOWLEDGMENTS

I should like to acknowledge valuable assistance from my colleagues, Professors Clayton Alderfer, Bliss Cartwright, Richard Hackman and Stanley Udy. Mrs Maryellen Holford was invaluable in typing and managing the production of the manuscript. Part of this book was originally presented at a symposium, 'Technology in Organizations of the Future', Department of Organizational Behavior, New York State School of Industrial and Labor Relations, Cornell University, 6–7 November 1970.

The author and publisher are also grateful to Professor Peter Blau and to the *American Sociological Review* for granting permission to reproduce figures 1, 2, 3 and 4.

PREFACE

During the past several years I have been especially involved in trying to understand some of the theoretical and applied problems of relating thought to effective action. This interest has led me to explore the degree to which our methods of rigorous research may, if used well, inhibit one from obtaining valid knowledge that could become the basis for effective action. I concluded that concepts of rigorous research may be identical to those that are used to design the assembly lines in large corporations. Subjects may react like workers and knowingly or unknowingly give invalid information (Argyris 1968). In short, the conceptions of rigorous research may be subject to question, as are the research procedures that are derived from these conceptions.

The next step was to look at examples of the knowledge produced by behavioral scientists to see how relevant they were to effective action and change. Explorations were completed of key theories and research in social psychology (Argyris 1969) and industrial psychology (1970a).

In the case of the former, dissonance and attribution theories were found to be applicable in the world as it now exists; a world dominated by low interpersonal trust and openness. The proponents of these theories have shown little interest, however, in exploring how behavioral science research could help to design and thus become appropriate to a world of high interpersonal trust and openness. It would not be surprising to learn that a reader, especially the lay practitioner, might conclude that in the present world dissonance and attribution activities are givens. They may therefore act to continue these activities. Thus these theories may help to form the basis for maintaining the *status quo*.

In the case of the latter an examination of industrial psychology suggested that many psychological researchers tended to place the environment (social structure, norms etc.), in a black box and act as if they did not exist or, if they did, were benign or trivial variables. The unintended consequences in the field of industrial psychology were (1) internally consistent and empirically valid theory were rarely developed, (2) the practical contributions ranged from being incomplete, to misleading, to dangerous, (3) the field accepted and reinforced the *status quo*, and therefore (4) produced much knowledge which was neither valid nor useful, (5) which may someday set the stage for society to decide to attempt to manage and re-orient the activities of industrial psychologists.

One day I received an invitation from Professor William Whyte to participate in a conference planned by Professor Ned Rosen and himself to explore issues emerging from recent empirical research in the field of sociology or organizations. He informed me that, among others, Professors Blau, Thompson, and Perrow had been invited and were planning to attend. I accepted the invitation with a strong sense of pleasure and gratitude. As I contemplated what I would write, it occurred to me that, in my inquiries about the relationship between thought and action, I always had difficulty with the work of these three renowned sociologists. All seemed to believe strongly in a 'sociological approach'. They were committed to developing theories about organizations that apparently ignored much of the research in personality, interpersonal relationships, and group dynamics.

As long as I was not concerned with the issue of effective action, then my bewilderment about how they could maintain, what seemed to me to be an unreal differentiation, never led to action on my part. After all, I kept saying to myself, all scholars have a right, indeed it is a necessity, to place limits and boundaries on their work. I, too, place boundaries in my work thereby making my work incomplete and lopsided.

However, once I became interested in the applicability of knowledge and in the idea that behavioral scientists ought to study organizations by creating new ones or changes in the existing ones, then the issue of where one drew the boundaries became very important. I had to confront myself and others about how we chose the variables we ignored.

In re-reading the work of these authors, I became even more convinced that their theories would tend to emulate and reinforce the *status quo, and* if an activist were to use these theories as a basis for change, he would become an authoritarian manipulator (again, the *status quo* in change processes). I also concluded that the exclusion of the variables listed above tended to make their sociological theory less effective.

I decided that one way to make the conference more of a learning experience for me and, at the same time, discuss some of the emerging questions, would be to raise the issues that concerned me by illustrating them with the work of Blau, Thompson, and Perrow. Not only were these scholars central figures in their respective fields; not only were they influencing many graduate students and others scholars; but, for my immediate purposes, they would have read the manuscript and could confront me directly on these issues.

As I began to write my paper, I decided to expand it to include other writers who were also active in the field but who expressed these sociological biases in different forms. I chose John Goldthorpe and David Lockwood because of their recent research and because it represents an approach that is somewhat different from Blau, Thompson and Perrow.

There are other sociologists whose works are similar and those whose works are dissimilar from these men. It seemed to me useful to note some of these people especially during the discussion of what might be done about these problems.

Part II, for several reasons, was not presented at the conference. Part I was already too long and common decency dictated that I ought not to impose myself on those present even more. But decency was not the only reason. The truth is my cognitive maps about these issues are not very clear. I believe that the framework developed so far, and presented in Part I is a useful one. However, I also see it as incomplete, its parts underdeveloped and as yet loosely connected. The primary reason for this is my lack of knowledge and my limitations. A secondary reason is the lack of research available, especially studies describing sociologists who attempt to test parts of theories by creating changes in on-going systems or organizations.

It was the questions of my fellow conferees and the enthusiastic encouragement and challenge of the younger faculty and graduate student observer-participants that led me to include my views on the subject even though they are primitive. Also, there is the hope that the material might stir up interest among scholars about the exacting intellectual problems involved in applying behavioral science knowledge effectively to the problems of our society as well as to redesigning it.

To Di, Dart and Dianne Ellen –
I love them all

1. PETER BLAU

Blau, acknowledging the existence of several foci of analysis in organizational research (individual and structure of social relations), has chosen to focus upon the system of interrelated elements that characterize the organization as a whole (Blau 1965, p. 325). 'The focus . . . is the system of interrelated elements that characterize the organization as a whole not its component parts' (Blau 1965, p. 326).

How does one study the whole without its component parts? The answer appears to be to study formal organization. The whole is therefore equated with the formal, intended aspects of organizations. Is there any research that helps to illuminate the difficulties in equating the whole with the formal organization? There are several, all of which suggest that the formal organization, no matter how clearly defined, rarely includes the whole organization. Arensberg and McGregor (1942), the Ohio State studies (1957), and Simon (1947) have shown that much human behavior cannot be understood by focussing on the formal organizational structure. More recently Woodward (1965, 1970) and her associates have emphasized the difficulty they found in obtaining organizational charts that were valid (their sample is now over 100 firms). Moreover, they reported that charts did not necessarily depict the important relationships. 'In some firms role relationships prescribed by the chart seemed to be of secondary importance to personal relationships between individuals' (Woodward 1965, p. 24). Perrow reported that he has had difficulties in getting top management to agree on such seemingly easy attributes of formal organizations as the number of levels. He concludes, 'We have been amazed at the nonchalance with which most researchers make their unexplained division of levels and can confidently report that one organization has five, whereas another has six or four . . . All criteria . . . charts, formal or informal; salary data . . . official level . . designations by the organizations; observations of department heads . . . had grave disadvantages' (Perrow 1970a, pp. 79–80). Blau himself has questioned the advisability of depending on formal charts and the understanding of formal procedures to understand behavior in organizations. 'Actually social interactions and activities in organizations never correspond perfectly to official prescriptions, if only because not all prescriptions are compatible, and there departures from the formal blueprint raise problems for empirical study. Paradoxically therefore although the defining characteristic of an organization is that a collectivity is formally organized, what makes it of scientific interest is that the developing social structure inevitably does not coincide completely with the pre-established forms' (Blau 1968, p. 298).

Thus we see when researchers, in studying organizations, have collected data depicting actual behavior, they have concluded that the formal organizations, at best, may represent the whole as it is *intended* but not the whole as it actually exists. If so, then why does Blau state that he is studying the organization as a whole by focussing on formal organization? We could find no discussion of this question.

Indeed, the Blau perspective may be even narrower if one asks the question how Blau operationally defines organizational intentions. Again because individual and group behavior at all levels are excluded, Blau operationally defines intentions as those of a few of the top management. Blau restricts himself 'to those data that can be obtained from the records of organizations and interviews with key informants, without intensive observation or interviewing' (Blau 1965, p. 333). Most of the information about formal structure comes from personnel lists, from elaborate charts specially prepared for the research, all of which were more detailed than the charts kept by the agencies (Blau 1970a, p. 204).

Why develop charts that are more detailed than those used by the organization in its daily work? One reason may be because, as pointed out above the formal charts do not describe the organization as it is; they describe it as it is intended to be. But if one wants to describe the organization as it is, then is there not some need to show empirically that what exists for the few senior managerial informants actually exists for the remainder of the organization? Webber has shown that superiors can distort their initiation of actions downward (Webber 1970).

Blau apparently does not believe that it is necessary to obtain empirical data to validate that the few may speak for the many. To do so would take him beyond the boundaries of his interests. The consequence, however, is to question the validity of his results.

An example of the difficulty that Blau creates for himself may be seen in his study of decentralization. Remaining consistent with his view he operationally measures the decentralization from the director and his deputy either to middle managers at the state headquarters or to managers of local offices, by obtaining the perceptions of 'several senior managers' (Blau 1970*b*, pp. 155–66). Blau assumes that several key top managers may speak validly for the remainder of the managerial organization, but never provides empirical evidence for this assumption. How is it possible to ignore the need for such empirical evidence in light of ample research that concludes that, in matters such as decentralization, superiors may not be valid informants of their subordinates' views? For example Greiner, Leitch and Barnes (1968) reported that significantly different perceptions existed among managers and technical people in variables that were related to the degree of centralization or decentralization participants experience (pp. 205–6). Sofer (1970) reported that the top management in two organizations were surprised 'that such a high proportion of men . . . felt that they were under-utilized, more than this, that their personal resources were rejected' (p. 9). Significant distortions have been reported on issues of decentralization and control among top management peers and between top management and their immediate subordinates (Argyris 1965, 1970). Indeed in one study it was shown that the distortive processes seemed to continue to the bottom of the managerial hierarchy (Argyris 1965).

CAUSAL EXPLANATIONS ARE OFFERED THAT ARE INCOMPLETE OR UNEXPLORED

A stated objective of Blau's work is to refine Weber's theory of bureaucracy. Blau agrees with Weber that specialization, administrative apparatus, hierarchy, and impersonal detachment are key characteristics of bureaucracy (Blau 1965, p. 333). He correctly points out that these characteristics exist in matters of degree and therefore can be dimensionalized. This, in turn, leads to quantitative studies where the degree of each characteristic may be correlated with the others or with other criterion variables.

After identifying the key characteristics of bureaucracy Blau also discusses their probable causality. He agrees with Weber that specialization is caused by the requirement to discharge complex responsibilities; that hierarchy is needed to effect the coordination of tasks and to enable supervisors to guide the performance of subordinates; that impersonal detachment is necessary to preclude the intrusion of such irrational elements (strong emotions and personal bias) as may interfere with rational decision making.

The moment Blau includes these generalizations in his theory, he involves the level of analysis that he has chosen to exclude. For example, why is specialization necessary or why does hierarchy lead to coordination and guidance? The answer may be found in any book on formal organization and partially in Blau's writings. Briefly, it goes something like this. According to engineering economics, *given the nature of people*, it is cheaper to specialize work. If people or units are specialized then they should make certain that they do what they are supposed to do. The way to control people and coordinate them is to give that job (a new speciality) to one individual and call him a supervisor. What makes him a supervisor? Among others things his authority to hire, fire, reward and penalize etc. Why give him these powers? Because, given what is known about people, these are ways to induce people to perform what the systems ask them to perform.

The point is that the basic design of the pyramidal structure is based on the properties of human beings. Specialization, power, hierarchy, follow because people are the basic unit. Thus the explanation for the primary characteristics of bureaucracy and whether they are effective or not does not exist independently of the nature of man. Indeed, it may be more accurate to say that they exist because of the properties of human beings. The formal organization is a cognitive strategy about how the designers intend that roles be played, given the nature of human beings. Excluding human beings from one's theoretical interest therefore excludes a host of variables that may be the key to understanding why formal organizations operate as they do, why they change, why they resist change, and how effective they may be.

CERTAIN CONDITIONS ARE IGNORED UNDER WHICH FORMAL ORGANIZATION MAY BE CHANGED BY THE PARTICIPANTS

The moment one includes in this theory statements suggesting that organizational effectiveness is intimately related to the degree of specialization, hierarchy, and impersonality etc., one's theory is open to examination on what it may say about the effectiveness of organizations. An important question regarding the relationship of effectiveness to specialization, hierarchy, and impersonality is how does one define when there is too much or too little of each of these variables. Can one derive, *from the theory*, hypotheses about such issues? One response is that specialization or hierarchy become 'too much' when they are overconstrictive and 'too little' when they do not influence the participants' behavior. But how does one decide when and why a dimension of bureaucracy is overconstrictive or uninfluential? Does not such a study require obtaining the perceptions of the participants, their tolerance toward constraints and structure etc.?

I do not believe that it is possible to derive *a priori* hypotheses about these issues or to make *ad hoc* explanations without including the nature of human beings in one's theory. Blau's human being is narrowly rational and obediently submissive to the organization. His man is reminiscent of economic man in microeconomics or administrative man in traditional scientific management.

Moreover, his conception places the responsibility upon management for the intelligence of the system, for its management, and for its change. Unless the proactive qualities of man are included, how will one be able to derive *a priori* the conditions and operationalize the points where organizational change is created by participants at different levels of the system? Is there not ample research to show that participants will create informal activities to counteract the formal and, in turn, that these informal activities may eventually become a cause of change of the formal structure and/or part of it? If one excludes these individual and group dimensions when one observes empirical variations in hierarchy, specialization, and impersonality, one may not be able to explain validly the variance; or one may develop generalizations that are invalid.

INVALID GENERALIZATIONS AND CONTRADICTORY EXPLANATIONS MAY GO UNNOTICED

To put the problem another way: since Blau excludes individual and group behavior from his theory, he also excludes it from his empirical research. Consequently the assumption that individual and group behavior can be ignored (for the problems Blau focusses upon) is never tested. The difficulties that follow from such a position may be illustrated from Blau's work. Blau agrees with Weber that impersonal detachment prevents irrational elements from affecting the decision-making processes. However, if one examines the research of individual and group behavior on this issue one will find that the way to reduce the irrational component in decision making is to identify the irrational elements in decisions and then rationally eliminate them. How can irrational components of decisions be eliminated unless they are observed and examined? (Argyris 1967, 1968). Hoopes' recent book (1969) on Vietnam or the articles on how the recent American massacres in Vietnam were kept hidden raise the question of the effectiveness of impersonal detachment. Reedy (1970) goes so far as to suggest that the effectiveness of the Presidency is seriously limited because few of the people around the President tell him all the facts. Cabinet meetings are formal, with a high degree of impersonality. An explosive issue is rarely discussed in full because it might violate the norm of impersonality. Recently Miller concluded that, '. . . contrary to Weber . . . a lack of impersonality may contribute to an organization's functioning. The quality of being well-liked . . . may contribute to the ability to exercise organizational control' (Miller 1970, p. 99).

Another example is related to Blau's operational measure of impersonality, namely the statistical records of the degree to which superior evaluates subordinate (Blau 1968, p. 335). The more frequent the contact the less the impersonality. Again, where individual and group behavior are actually studied one finds that this assumption is not necessarily valid. For example, Meyer, Kay and French (1965) have presented empirical evidence of what actually goes on during meetings where the superior evaluates the subordinate. They found stronger feelings of mistrust and impersonality after the meeting than before. Thus it was possible for people to feel increased impersonal detachment as a result of increased interactions. However, this was not true in all cases. In some cases, the contact actually did create increased feelings of closeness and loss of detachment. Given Blau's theory and research strategy, the former findings would be unpredictable and the latter impossible to test. However, these findings are crucial to the kinds of predictions Blau is making and the generalizations he is producing.

A similar problem exists for the measurement of hierarchy. Hierarchy, Blau states, is needed to effect coordination of diverse tasks by enabling superiors on successive levels to guide, directly or indirectly, the performance of subordinates (Blau 1965, p. 334). The operational measures used are: (1) the number of levels, (2) the average span of control, and (3) the proportion of personnel in managerial positions. The logic Blau assumes is that the more favorable the span of control etc., the more effective will be the coordination and the direct or indirect guidance. But there are no data presented to illustrate that this, in fact, is the case. Such data are needed, especially since empirical data exist that, in order to study coordination, direction and control accurately, one must also study the manner in which they are actually performed (Likert 1967). Also, how would Blau's measures explain the findings of Argyris (1960) and Goldthorpe *et al.* (1968) that effective supervision existed (for middle and lower level managers and for employees) as long as the former left the latter alone? That is, effective supervision and coordination were occurring when it was not being done.

The same difficulties arise when Blau asserts that larger units contain a comparatively large number of employees in nearly every occupational speciality, thereby providing a congenial ingroup of colleagues for most employees (often not available in small organizations) and they simultaneously enhance opportunities for stimulating contacts with people whose training and experience are unlike their own (1970*b*, p. 200). In one study of a large central bank there was little congenial interaction reported within groups and little or no interest evidenced by employees to learn other jobs. In the small branch banks however, employees developed congenial relationships across occupational specialities and because of group cohesion individuals learned each other's jobs in order to be of help so that all could finish work about the same time (Argyris 1954). The point again is that Blau is assuming a certain conception of man, one who, for example, prefers congenial relations with those with similar occupational interests. Further, he assumes that a heterogeneity of occupational interests leads to interest in widening one's repertoire of skills. One wishes that he would make more explicit this conception of man because it does not fit with the empirical findings available.

Finally, Blau gets into difficulty when he states that his findings may negate Merton's view that formalization of procedures leads to increased rigidity and eventually less decentralization (Blau 1970*b*, p. 160). Blau reports that 'strict adherence to civil service standards in making appointments as well as the elaboration of formalized personnel regulations promotes decentralization which implies a less rigid structure of decision making' (Blau 1970*b*, p. 160).

There are at least two reasons to question the assertion that Merton has been disproven. Firstly a methodological reason: if the measures of decentralization are what a few top people say exist, then all Blau found was that strict adherence to civil service standards and elaboration of formalized personnel regulations led the few senior informants to believe there was greater decentralization. This generalization says nothing about what the remainder of the management experience and as such does not necessarily negate Merton's hypothesis which could apply to organizational rigidity as experienced by more than a few key people.

We may also ask why key top level informants perceive greater decentralization with strict adherence to civil service standards and elaboration of formalized personnel regulations. One possibility is that they now feel free to let subordinates do the hiring precisely because strict adherence and elaborate formalized regulations lock the subordinate into what the superior wants. The subordinate can now make a decision because the superior believes he has him programmed to make the decision as he (superior) would or, if this is not the case, he can throw the regulations at him.

Is this decentralization? At one level of analysis it is: subordinates instead of superiors are hiring people. At another level it may not be because the subordinates may not feel they have greater control; they may feel that they are carrying out the orders from the top. The second level asks, if there are formal procedures that give subordinates opportunities to hire, how do the subordinates view these opportunities? Do they experience these opportunities to hire as a sign of decentralization and flexibility or do they experience it as a sign of pseudo-decentralization and rigidity? Blau has, by the theory and the empirical measures used, ruled out these kinds of questions in his study of decentralization.

Blau appears to compound the difficulties by going on to make normative statements, based on his findings, about how people in organizations may be managed more effectively. He begins by asking why the elaboration of formalized personnel procedures into an extensive body of written regulations furthers decentralization (Blau 1970*b*, p. 163). He answers that

the requirement to conform to a simple set of personnel

regulations has the disadvantage that these standards become a straitjacket into which must be forced all kinds of different cases in a large variety of situations . . . one way to deal with the many exceptional cases not adequately covered by a simple set of rules is to permit officials to depart from these rules at their discretion, but doing so undermines the important advantages that following personnel standards provides to the organization. An alternative method for coping with a large variety of cases and situations is to devise appropriate personnel standards for each type, supplemented by additional rules specifying under what conditions which standards are to be applied. This elaborating of the system of personnel regulations preserves the advantage resulting from compliance with merit standards of appointments and simultaneously avoids the disadvantage for personnel-selection resulting from either rigid application of inappropriate standards or idiosyncratic departures from standards.

Blau asserts that giving officials discretion to handle a variety of cases undermines the personnel standards and that elaborate systems of merit standards are more efficient. This may be the case but no empirical data are included that show that 'giving officials discretion . . . undermines personnel standards' or that 'elaborate systems of merit standards are more efficient'. If one has no data and one wishes to make statements like these, then is one not responsible for exploring the relevant behavioral literature? – most of which, by the way, would not support this view. Moreover, if one were to collect data would not one need a concept of efficiency? From what point of view are elaborate systems more efficient? This sounds very much like a statement from a traditional management theorist. Is this the criterion Blau wishes to utilize?

If one examines Blau's statement about decentralization above, one will find that he argues for such a complete set of rules that individual discretion becomes minimal. How is this an explanation of decentralization? One way to make the logic consistent is to assume that the act of hiring an individual is more of an index of decentralization than what behavior actually is manifested during that act. As a minimum, are we not owed evidence for this assumption?

Blau is, in actuality, making important assumptions about the nature of human beings and what they experience as decentralization. This concept implies that a man can experience a sense of influence and control in certain decisions (a criterion of decentralization) when the only choice he has is to behave strictly according to precisely defined regulations. Is it too extreme to ask that if such an individual existed he might not be classified as mildly distorted?

DIFFICULTIES IN FORMALIZING ORGANIZATIONAL THEORY

Recently, Blau has published a major paper whose objective is the development of a formal theory of formal organizations (Blau 1970a). There are some difficulties with the theory that are relatable to the problem described above.

Let us begin with Blau's statement that he wishes to develop a deductive theory of formal organizations focussing on the process of differentiation within organizations, be it spatial, occupational, hierarchical, or functional. The theory is limited to major antecedents and consequences of structural differentiation. It has been derived from the empirical results of a study of the social forces that govern the interrelations among differentiated elements in the formal structure. It ignores the psychological and group and intergroup forces which govern behavior (Blau 1970a, p. 210).

How does Blau go about developing such a study? Researchers in the field study fifty-three employment security agencies by obtaining organizational charts, interviewing several key top informants, reading personnel and organizational policy manuals. Next, special formal organizational charts are developed. Then the basic dimensions of bureaucracy are dimensionalized and appropriate correlational analyses made and certain statistical curves are developed. On the basis of these empirical findings, two generalizations are formulated and given the status of axioms from which derivations are made. They are:

(1) Increasing size generates structural differentiation in organizations along various dimensions at decelerating rates (Blau 1970a, p. 204).

(2) Structural differentiation in organizations enlarges the administrative component (Blau 1970a, p. 212).

In order to explore these generalizations, we should go back to the beginning, namely to the choice of the organization made. First, the civil service organizations studied operated under conditions that could have affected the forces of differentiation, be they spatial, occupational, hierarchical, or functional. For example:

(1) All the organizations existed in a world where budgets had been and continue to be tight. The very tightness of funds may influence the number of people an agency may hire and thus the levels of organization.

(2) The civil service operates under rules that make it increasingly difficult to obtain slots for increasingly higher positions. Thus the higher the position sought, the more pressure against it being created, funded, and filled.

(3) The organizations studied have a finite 'marketing' terrain. Each state or local agency is clearly limited to prescribed geographical conditions and to the range of services that can be offered.

(4) All the systems have approached or have reached their prescribed limits.[1]

Second, civil service organizations represented a population of organizations that have tended to adhere most rigorously to the traditional formal organizational theory. Consequently, they may not allow the degrees of freedom necessary for testing rival hypotheses. One may argue that Blau and his associates could conduct studies in other types of organizations to reduce this danger. I would agree but point out that a subsequent study (apparently carried out by Blau and his associates) also represents a civil service population. This issue becomes especially pertinent because it has been shown that organizational forms vary as much within a sample of organizations performing similar objectives as among twenty-five organizations with different objectives. Apparently the structure was influenced by the nature of the organizational politics (Kaufman and Seidman 1970).

However, even if this problem were ultimately overcome there is a third problem which is more basic. As mentioned above, civil service organizations are designed directly from such organizational principles as task specialization, span of control, and unity of command etc. As employees are hired they are, in accordance with unity of command and task specialization, grouped together into a functional unit. Given the notion of chain of command each unit has to have a boss. Given span of control each boss may

[1] Blau acknowledges number four (he states his theory may not apply to emergent systems) and partially number one (he states that budgets cannot be open-ended; there are limits to funds available).

supervise a certain number of subordinates. As the organization grows larger the number of units increases and so does the number of bosses increase, but given the span of control regulations, so does the need to coordinate the bosses. So we have super bosses.

But super bosses are difficult to obtain because they cost more and their slots are centrally managed. Also, given budgetary limitations additional employee help may be obtained if a given superior is willing to squeeze him under his control; or a given superior is willing to squeeze another unit under his control. Both of these forces would act to decrease the forces for expansion as the organization grew larger.

The point is that the findings Blau reported were *not* generated or caused by size alone. The causes of the curves that he produces include the principles of task specialization, unity of command, span of control, budgetary limitations, rules about super-lend appointments, the current political climate between the agencies and government etc. *Size may be correlated with, but may not be said to generate or to cause, structural differentiation.* To put this another way, the results Blau obtained from his study of the organizational charts might have been dramatically different if the basic managerial theory was one of project management and matrix organizations.

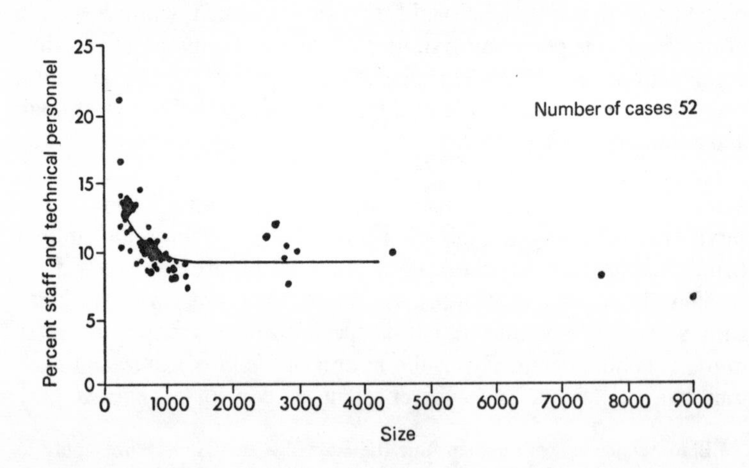

Figure 1. Size of agency and percent staff personnel

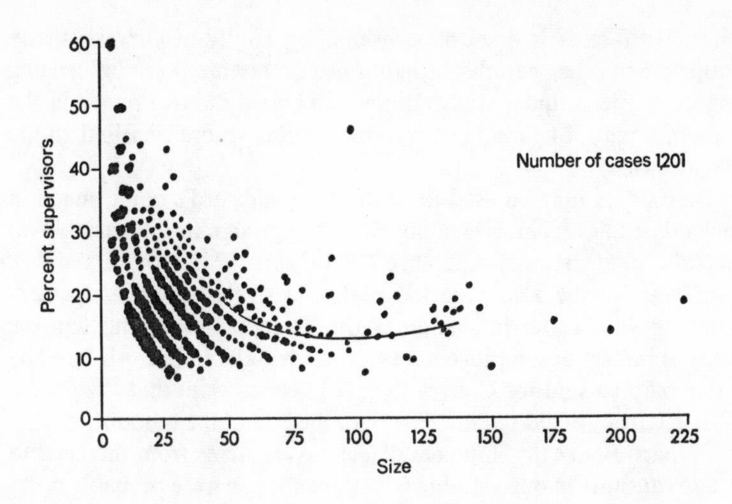

Figure 2. Size of local office and percent supervisory personnel

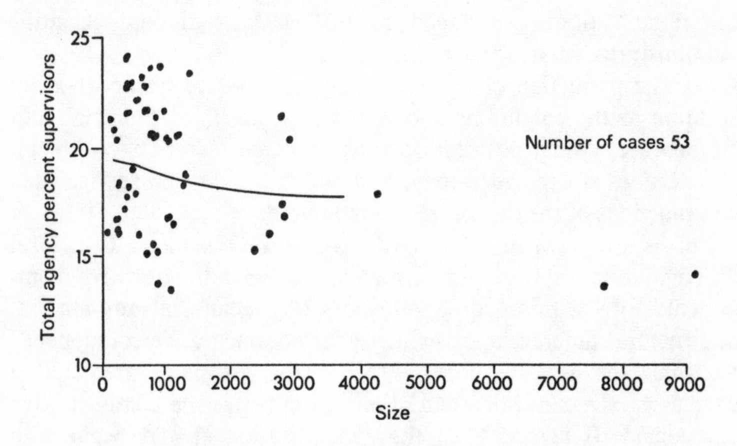

Figure 3. Size of agency and percent supervisory personnel in total agency

Given this interpretation, some of Blau's attempts to draw curves from his findings become more understandable. First, is it unfair to ask if Blau has not stretched the imagination a bit to develop his curves? The curve in figure 1 depends a lot on the three organizations at 4,000, nearly 8,000 and 9,000 points. Figure 2 is not one curve. In fact, it is a set of a fascinating family of curves usually found when other variables (than those represented) are influencing the phenomena under study. If one eliminated the two points in the extreme right of figure 3 one can draw a circle more clearly than the line drawn.

Blau's data may be used to illustrate Woodward's point, made in several studies, that size alone was *not* a significant variable to explain organizational difference (Woodward 1965, pp. 31 and 40). Incidentally, she also reported that 'the size of the management group gave a better indication of the "bigness" of a firm than the total number of employees' (Woodward 1965, pp. 41–2). The same may be said for Coleman's (1961) conclusion, that the degree of specialization did not increase with the size of the school.

Perhaps Blau's development of the curves stems from the need to relate causality to one variable (size) when many were probably operating, thereby giving the actual scatter obtained. If this analysis has merit then Blau's first proposition should be rewritten as follows:

(1) Increasing the number of employees i*s correlated* with structural differentiation in organizations along various dimensions *if* the organization is designed in line with traditional scientific (administrative) management principles.

(2) The prediction of decelerating rates tends to occur when, in addition to the conditions above, budgets are finite, financial constraints are strong, position openings become increasingly difficult as one goes up the hierarchy, and the marketing or service area and functions of the organization are limited.

Let us now turn to the second major generalization. 'Structural differentiation in organizations enlarges the administrative component.' First a minor question. Does this mean that any amount of structural differentiation enlarges the administrative component? I assume the negative because to do otherwise is to predict that decreasing structural differentiation . . . enlarges the administrative component. If agreed, then the generalization should begin with the word 'increasing'.

Now to the more important points. Let us explore the operational definitions for structural differentiation and administrative component. The administrative component is a distinct official status like a supervisor or a sub unit like a branch. Structural differentiation is any criterion on the basis of which members are formally divided into ranks or sub units. Thus one criterion for structural differentiation is units, but each unit has a supervisor. But supervisors are an operational definition of an administrative component. The findings therefore are: increasing structural differentiation by increasing the number of supervisors or units (each of whom by definition has a supervisor) increases the number of units that have supervisors. Do we not have a tautology depending upon what measures are used for administrative components?

Moreover, the second generalization is stated as an axiom because, states Blau, as organizations are differentiated, problems of coordination and communications intensify (Blau 1970a, p. 213). What are the data Blau presents for this causal explanation? If I read him correctly, he did not collect data on this issue. Indeed the variables involved were not measured in the research; they were inferred (Blau 1970a, p. 213). Implicit in the process of inference are, according to Blau, the following assumptions:

(1) Differentiation makes an organization more complex.

(2) Complex structures engender problems of communication and coordination.

(3) These problems, in turn, cause resistance to further differentiation.

(4) Line supervisors at all levels have to spend more time dealing with these problems.

(5) Line supervisors have less time to review the work of the subordinates, hence more supervisors are needed.

Hence, the more differentiated the formal structure, the more administrative personnel should be found in an organization of a given size and the narrower the span of control of the supervisors and managers. But Blau defines 'differentiated' by functional units. Since every unit must have a boss (given chain of command), you should find more administrative personnel. Moreover, if you have more bosses and hold size constant, then of course the span of control will be narrowed (Blau 1970a, p. 213). What is Blau's theory telling us that goes beyond the traditional management theory?

Finally, if plans are developed to study the five assumptions above, how will human communication, coordination, resistance, and leadership be studied without including individual and group behavioral variables? What is the nature of the theoretical inheritance that Blau offered those who may choose to follow his work?

A QUALITY CONTROL ON CIVIL SERVICE OPERATING MANUALS

If one examines closely the recent work of Blau and Schoenherr (1970, in press) from which the article above was derived, one will find, as stated above, that many of the generalizations offered already exist in the literature because they stem from the study of civil service rules which, in turn, are derived directly from the work of traditional administrative theorists. For example:

(1) Scope (or volume of responsibility) is correlated 0.98 with the number of employees (p. 72).

Why would this not be the case since, given formal organization principles, volume of responsibility is directly created by the number of employees?

(2) The larger an agency is, the greater the number of job titles, hierarchical levels, number of major divisions etc. (p. 73).

Again, given the formal organizational principles used by the civil service, the only way an agency can get larger is to increase the job titles, hierarchical levels, which, in turn, necessarily (because of span of control) increases the number of major divisions.

(4) 'The interpretation advanced is that hierarchical differentiation into multiple levels tends to occur in large organizations because it relieves top management of excessive supervisory burdens that interfere with its basic executive responsibility' (p. 93).

Why is this 'interpretation advanced' by the author? Hierarchical differentiation into multiple levels is an inevitable consequence in organizations because of such principles as chain of command, span of control, and authority should be commensurate with responsibility, defined by Urwick, Gulick and others.

One could make the point in another way. Blau and his associates, by developing generalizations similar to or consonant with the ones already in the civil service regulations, have provided evidence that the agencies are organized largely in accordance with civil service regulations. They have performed a quality control check on the line managements throughout the agency.

Where will this analysis lead? As Simon (1947) has pointed out, principles of scientific management are not principles and cannot be tested (in terms of effectiveness) because they do not contain criterion variables. Perhaps this is why Blau and Schoenherr state early that they are not interested in focussing on effectiveness issues. But do they mean to offer a theory that no one can use to answer questions of effectiveness? If not, then it would be helpful if they could give some clues how effectiveness studies might be made.

Actually Blau and Schoenherr do get involved in effectiveness issues throughout their manuscript but do not provide any insights that go beyond those already in the literature of public administration and the civil service regulations. For example they state: 'A tall hierarchy has the advantage of reducing top management's administrative load, but at the same time, the disadvantages of increasing its distance from operating levels' (p. 94). The advantage and disadvantages mentioned by Blau and Schoenherr are stated in the literature. The statement carries with it the questions raised years ago. For example, how do Blau and Schoenherr know that a tall hierarchy actually reduces top management's load? They also state: 'The more top management relies on impersonal mechanisms of control . . . the less of a liability is the tall hierarchy' (p. 94). Again, how do they know this? Did they make any observations? Apparently not. Did they interview the subordinates down the line who were involved? Apparently not.

INTERRELATIONSHIPS WITH OTHER THEORIES OF FORMAL ORGANIZATIONS

There are, at least, two other theories about why formal organizations arise and develop as they do, which someday will need to be accounted for by Blau's theory of formal organization. The difficulty is that both theories are based upon the authors' conception of man, the dimensions excluded by Blau.

The first theory is Simon's. He suggests that formal organizational structures arise because they represent the very way man thinks and solves problems. Man's thinking mechanisms naturally lead him to specialization and hierarchy (Simon 1969). Blau's view that 'Simon's theory is really not one of organization', that (Simon) 'takes for granted the conditions in the organization' and that Simon ignores the central problem of organizational structure does not seem to be accurate (Blau 1968, p. 302). Indeed one may argue that Simon has shown as much, if not a more basic, interest in organizational structure because he has attempted to provide a rigorous theory of how and why it arises. Blau may question the theory but why does he apparently choose to rule it out? I suggest because he is committed to ignoring the individual level of analysis.

Blau and his associates will also have to confront another recent view of formal organizations suggested by Jaques. He implies that 'hierarchical pyramidal organizations . . . [reflect] the character and distribution of human capacity' (Jaques 1964, p. 8).

Jaques' theory has to be dealt with by Blau because one of its major derivations is that organizational growth may be conceptualized in two different ways. One is growth simply by an increase in numbers of employees, and if necessary, by adding extra managerial commands. If the point is reached where managers become overburdened as a result of having too many subordinates, then additional sections of the same kind may be set up under newly appointed managers (Jaques 1964, p. 14). The other type of growth occurs when the organization has somehow reached the limit of its existing pattern, and must differentiate itself by taking on new hierarchical state with a significantly different time span. Blau's findings are based on the former concept of growth. If the latter is a valid one, then the two will require eventual integration.

SUMMARY

Our analysis suggests

(1) Although Blau states that he is studying organizations as wholes, he does not present a conceptual or operational definition of this view of reality. It may be more accurate to say that he is studying only a part of organization, or organizations without formal or informal subdivisions.

(2) The focus is primarily on formal organization. This aspect of organizations has been shown to be incomplete and varying in form depending upon whose view one gets. Blau's primary data sources are highly biased toward top management view.

(3) Blau's work may be more properly viewed as a quality control check on civil service regulations than as a contribution to new formal organizational theory.

(4) The way the data are gathered could lead to contamination by the influence of leadership style, administrative controls, interpersonal relations, group dynamics and intergroup relations. Since none of these is studied, their influence is neither known nor defined.

(5) Frequently explanations for correlational findings are developed that utilize or depend upon the variables that have been excluded (e.g. those listed in the previous conclusions).

(6) Since the directly observable behavior of individuals, groups or intergroup is not studied, the measures develop difficulties. For example, what is decentralization in the eyes of top management can be centralization for the subordinates. Also the criteria used to define impersonality and its converse are not adequate since impersonality can be created under the conditions that are defined for the converse.

(7) There is no apparent way of generating insights about innovation in present organizations or generating new organizational forms that take into account the nature of man and of the group.

(8) There are key generalizations that may be tautological.

2. JAMES THOMPSON

Thompson has developed a theory of 'organizations in the round' which is composed of a few basic and well interrelated concepts. His objective is to understand what truly constitutes organized social activity; he wishes to identify the distinctive properties of organization (Thompson 1967).

THE NATURE OF ORGANIZATIONS

Thompson, quoting Gouldner (1959), believes that the organizational literature contains two underlying models of organization. They are the 'rational' and 'natural' systems models. Scientific management, administrative management and bureaucracy are examples of the rational closed-system approach. Combined they emphasize: (1) economic efficiency as ultimate criterion, (2) planning, setting standards, and control, (3) specializing tasks, and larger units, (4) chain of command and span of control, and (5) experts, rules, and rewards and penalties. Closed-systems logic is determinate because everything is functional, 'making a positive, indeed an optimum contribution to the result. All resources are appropriate resources and their allocation fits a master plan. All action is appropriate action, and its outcome is predictable. Planning and controlling are its major activities' (Thompson 1967, p. 6).

The natural system model assumes that organizations are more complex and that their behavior cannot easily be controlled or predicted. The whole is created by a 'set of interdependent parts . . . and each contributes something and receives something from the whole, which in turn is interdependent with some larger environment' (Thompson 1970, p. 6). 'The natural system model stresses homeostasis or self-stabilization, which spontaneously or naturally governs the necessary relationships among parts and activities and thereby keeps the system viable in the face of disturbances stemming from the environment' (Thompson 1970, p. 7).

Thompson places much emphasis on the distinction that the

closed-system is not based upon uncertainty and that the natural-system model is based upon uncertainty.

THE ENVIRONMENT IS THE KEY TO UNCERTAINTY

Thompson focusses on the uncertainty as caused by the technology and by the external environment. The scientific management and administrative theories, which he describes as based on certainty, have actually focussed upon the uncertainty of the internal environment. They have assumed that if the internal organization were managed effectively it would be tuned correctly into the requirements of the technology and the environment. Why and how this was so has not been spelled out by these theorists. Nevertheless, it is not accurate to describe them as unaware of uncertainty; they simply focussed on a source of uncertainty which Thompson largely ignores. Why else would they focus so heavily on planning and controlling (as Thompson admits) if it was not to overcome the uncertainty possible within the system?

Thompson's discussion of open systems states that a system is open if it is interdependent with the environment. Open systems, he continues, depend upon the environment for their inputs and for selling their outputs. The difficulty with this definition of open system is that it misses the central role of the internal environment. It is possible for a system to be aware of its interdependence with the environment and to choose to ignore it (Michael 1968). The explanation for such a choice would not be possible without focussing on the internal processes.

For example, the U.S. State Department has literally hundreds of documents emphasizing the importance of, and its interdependence with, the environment outside the United States. Indeed, foreign (environmental) affairs is its central concern. Yet there is some preliminary research that suggests that the system is becoming increasingly closed; ineffective in sensing accurately its environment (Argyris 1967). The result is that, according to one undersecretary, it has become a 'fudge factory'. If one examines the forces leading to these difficulties, they are largely located in the internal make-up of the system.

The point is that openness is only partially related to the system's awareness of the environment. Openness is also related to the internal make-up. Moreover, in the case of the State Department, the primary internal forces causing the closedness were interpersonal and intergroup relations. These are precisely the factors that Thompson has chosen to exclude.

Finally, as pointed out at the outset, Thompson identifies the informal activities as part of the natural system. The natural system, according to Gouldner and Thompson, is a flexible and open system. It may be seen as a counter reaction to the rigidity of the formal system, but Thompson would suggest that it is basic, not simply derivative. However, if one recalls the work of Whyte, Dalton, and Collins on worker informal activities, one will note that they possessed many of the properties of the formal-closed system. For example, rate busting and rate setting had economics as the ultimate criterion, employees set standards and controlled through their own informal chain of command; rules, rewards and penalties were designed to keep people 'in line'.

THOMPSON'S VIEW OF THE NEW TRADITION

One might wish to argue, however, that these points are trivial since Thompson argues for some combination of the closed- and open-system approach. He cites the Simon–March–Cyert work as an example of the new tradition. Search and learning and decision making become key concepts with the organizations admitting their bounded rationality and seeking a satisfying result.

The question arises, how different is this approach in terms of the dimensions Thompson has defined as being characteristic of open and closed systems? Returning to his criteria of closed system, and comparing with the Cyert and March work, one begins to wonder. What concepts of effectiveness do these authors include that go beyond the economic, closed-system view of organizations? If one followed their theorizing the level of the participants' aspiration would be altered from the possibility of maximizing or optimizing to satisfying. They also have increased the role of search in their theory. However, although these changes go somewhat beyond the criteria related to economics they remain well within the traditional view of management (Bower 1970). Planning, setting standards and control, for example, are key activities in their view. Indeed, their models are early examples of what could (and may have already) become sophisticated management information systems. Such systems seek not only to plan and control the formal activities; they seek to plan and control all activities. Their power to create conditions of psychological failure, reduction of space of free movement, a sense of helplessness and hopelessness is greater than anything the traditional theorists could develop (Argyris 1971a). Moreover Cyert and March do not alter the specialization of tasks, of units, the chain of command etc. Indeed, they would bring in new experts, develop many more rules, quantify them in order to make the pyramidal structure work more economically and efficiently. Their book represents an example of how man can use knowledge about human motivation (e.g. levels of aspiration, psychological inducements, and cognitive processes) in order to manage men much more completely.

This point may be illustrated by examining the Thompson view of efficiency. Organizations exhibit three distinct levels of responsibility and control. They are technical, managerial and institutional. Thompson believes that technology and the environment are major sources of uncertainty for organizations. One way an organization attempts to deal with uncertainty is to behave rationally at the technical level. Technical rationality is evaluated by two criteria: instrumental and economic. The former asks if the specified actions do in fact produce the desired outcome. The latter asks if the results are obtained with the least necessary expenditures (Thompson 1970, p. 14).

Here we note the beginnings of what appears to be a major inconsistency. Thompson begins his theory by saying that he intends to integrate the formal and the natural systems model. The latter he (partially) defines as the informal activities. Informal activities recreated by human beings to help make the formal organization more 'livable' while they get on with the tasks assigned to them. Thus an integration of these two models would presumably require the development of a third criterion for the 'new' concept of rationality, namely one that includes 'human costs'. We note that Cyert and March do not seem to have any such concept. Now it appears as if Thompson is also excluding it.

The response may be that the human cost dimensions are included because 'expenditure of resources' could include human resources, as it does in the case of Likert (1967). If this were the case then is not one required to do what Likert does, namely to develop a concept of the human being, a concept of the organization that could be congruent with his model of man and then develop an accounting system that integrates human and non-human costs? Why does Thompson not give much attention to this task? He would respond that this was not his job. But why not? I believe it is because of his implicit view of the nature of man. It is not much different from the one used by Cyert and March. The latter have developed a richer cognitive view of man than was the case of traditional management theory. However, man the human being, with feelings, needs, defenses, interpersonal relations, group dynamics, is beyond their theory. Consequently, they do not focus on developing an operational measure of human costs.

THOMPSON'S VIEW OF THE NATURE OF MAN

For example, let us look at what Thompson has chosen to emphasize when he discusses, 'the variable human'. He cites that man brings to work aspirations, standards and beliefs about causation. There is no discussion about how these factors are developed, maintained or enlarged. There is no discussion of how man can use these to mold or influence his environment. Indeed, by Thompson's definition of the closed-system, man is the most closed of all, excepting the one set of influences, namely the 'homogenizing influence of culture and organizations'. Thompson admits that there must be variation in human abilities and needs but he is not going to focus on these issues. He believes it is more important to focus on the socialization processes by which man is molded into the resources the organization needs. This is consistent with his view that organizational behavior is dominated by norms of rationality. But what are the processes by which human beings are 'homogenized' by systems? One thinks one will get them when he arrives at a section on inducements and contributions and how man is induced to work. However, all we learn is that there are inducements which, if effective, can cause the individual to contribute to the organization.

In the chapter immediately after the 'variable human' the concept of discretion is discussed. Perhaps here one may find something more about man as an open system; to paraphrase Thompson, man in the round. Unfortunately this is not the case. Man is again cognitive man, focussing on playing games with rules related to games theory. This is followed by a discussion of (1) how and when man will evade discretion, (2) how organizations sometimes thwart discretion, (3) how organizations may bias discretion through reward and penalties, and (4) how they police against deviant discretion. Note all these are 'pessimistic', constraining views of the problem. It is either how man avoids discretion or how organizations inhibit and bias the expression of distortion... In addition to man being conceived as a relatively closed reactive system, the organization is seen as the all-controlling all-powerful system. There can be no objection to this emphasis, as long as it can be shown to be consistent with the rest of the theory and it can be shown eventually to be more effective than competing views. As to the latter, it is an empirical question and awaits (1) further research designed specially to test aspects of the theory or (2) reviews of other research to show that this theory gives a more parsimonious explanation than competing theories.

As to the former, I question if this position is consistent with the demands of the theory as it is presently conceived. Thompson states explicitly that he is interested in the natural, spontaneous, less predictable aspects of organization. How can these factors be understood without including the informal activities? These activities arise *not* so much when the organization is homogenizing the individual but rather when the individual is reshaping the organization. Thompson's view of man is that he is rational and the rational behavior (as long as one gets paid for it) is to permit oneself to be socialized as the organization requires. The individual is not seen as active, initiative-taking, or organization-changing. Will not such a position miss a good deal of the causes of the natural, spontaneous, and less predictable?

My second reason for questioning the adequacy of Thompson's view of man for the requirements of his own theory relates to how the organization becomes aware of, and remains in effective contact with, its environment. One important set of factors is the administrative controls, long-range planning activities, and environment-sensing procedures an organization has designed (which would be included by Thompson). A second set of factors is how individuals, especially at the top, utilize, interpret, and act on the incoming information. Research of top management groups suggests that the amount of conformity, risk-taking, openness, destructiveness, intergroup crisis, management crisis, and trust are all critical in the way individuals search, understand, and ultimately manipulate the system to adapt it to its environment (Argyris 1965, 1968). However, these factors are all excluded in all the formal propositions defined by Thompson. But one cannot guarantee that these factors are not operating by excluding them from the study. Since these would not be variables that Thompson would include in his research, how will he ever know that the factors he includes are the only ones that make a difference in the way a system maintains its openness with the environment?

THOMPSON'S VIEW AND ENGINEERING ECONOMICS

I should like to suggest that Thompson's theory is less an integration of the formal and natural systems models and much more an explication of scientific management and engineering economics. There are several ways to illustrate this hypothesis.

(1) All the propositions are hypothesized as being valid under conditions of norms of rationality. What is rationality? It is a state where one can plan for, and predict relatively accurately, the effective operation and survival of the system. What are the criteria of effectiveness? Instrumental (does it produce what is intended?) and economic (does it do it with the least expenditure of money?). Are these two criteria not at the heart of the traditional formal management theories, be they scientific management, administrative management or bureaucracy?

(2) The design described by Thompson is basically a pyramidal structure. Concepts of vertical integration, increasing sales, minimizing costs, are an integral part of traditional management theories and theories of engineering economics. We are told that organizations employing long-linked technologies and subject to rationality norms seek to expand their domain through vertical integration. How far does this take us beyond the present writings of traditional organizational experts? The concept of vertical integration has been discussed as early as 1899 by engineers and managers (Chandler 1962, pp. 33–4). This point is made less to question the newness of Thompson's position than to emphasize that some of the propositions Thompson develops come from industrial engineering and are vaguely related to social science. Moreover, in recent decades there are new and much more sophisticated models being developed by micro-economists that have taken industrial engineering out of their intellectual dark ages. If Thompson wishes to focus on this intellectual lineage then perhaps he should explore the more

recent writings in the field. For example financial models have been developed that tell us more than Thompson implied when he stated that vertical integration is not simply a historical phenomenon, but a rational reaction to shrinking profit margins which, in turn, leads to the desire to eliminate significant contingencies. The reason Thompson gave that it would occur was that the organization would expand by keeping its present type of technology. But do the economic models predict this consequence? What are the economic processes that lead one to predict the 'inside' long-linked technology as the best with expansion?

Similar questions may be asked about the prediction that organizations employing mediating technologies will expand by increasing the population served. This is true by definition since 'mediating technologies' are defined in terms of populations being served. What is needed is to go beyond what is true by definition. For example, an organization of this type could expand by increasing the range of its services. (Also is it true that by increasing the population served one 'reduced contingencies'?) The now famous Cornfield financial investment operation is an example where they did this and eventually led to its collapse. People had lost confidence in management. Perhaps administrative competence of individuals, groups or the organization as a whole is a very relevant variable. Indeed, under certain conditions more important than technology and environment. Why is this not included in the theory? Could not one argue that it is a crucial component in keeping the system an open system?

Another area in which it would be helpful to see the theory develop some propositions is related to the 'balancing' of the different types of technologies (since many organizations have several different types of technologies). Thompson begins this with the proposition that such organizations will seek to grow until the least reducible component is approximately fully occupied (Thompson 1967, p. 1). Here is where we need much more theory and data. On the theory side, we need to have included the formulas from engineering economics or micro-economics which show that this step, better than any other one, is the predictable one (as defined by Thompson). On the data side, how does Thompson deal with organizations which choose to leave their least reducible component economically ineffectively occupied and expand by buying new companies? (Lobb and Ellis 1970).

(3) Propositions are given where it is explicitly assumed that management behaves rationally to establish clear goals and minimize economic costs. Indeed most managements strive to behave this way. And if this is all one can say, one cannot distinguish between those that provide service and those that are interested primarily in profit. One needs to include much more sophisticated views of the internal workings of the organization, along economic and human dimensions. Examples of how the latter greatly influences the former may seem to be dramatically in the area of acquisitions and disinvestments. A recent study shows that many human factors inhibit top management from acting according to 'norms of rationality'. According to two finanical experts, the creative divestitures are in the minority. The reasons, they note, are 'illogical and non-economic'. For example (1) successful executives are embarrassed to admit past mistakes or (2) they become identified with 'their baby' which leads many (3) to become stubborn and develop false hopes for a brighter tomorrow, thereby hiding (4) their basic fears of change or (5) their sentimentality (this was one of the original products) (Lobb and Ellis 1970).

(4) There is the implicit inclusion into the theory of variables that are explicitly excluded. For example, the proposition that 'under norms of rationality organizations group positions to minimize coordination costs' (Thompson 1967, p. 57). This is true if management acts in accordance with the view that they prefer man to be under control. This preference implies certain assumptions about man which McGregor (1960) has called theory *X*. There are organizations today that are increasing costs of coordination in order to increase innovation and flexibility. This is the major assumption of matrix organizations (Argyris 1967).

Also, 'under norms of rationality assessors prefer efficiency over instrumental tests and instrumental tests over social tests' (Thompson 1967, p. 87). This proposition is a near tautology since 'norms of rationality' are defined in terms of efficiency and instrumental tests. Social tests were not included under the concept of rationality, yet today they are becoming increasingly rational. The proposition assumes a cognitive economic-oriented man who will go toward instrumental tests only if the economics tests are not available. Why does he prefer the economics tests? Because 'where efficiency tests are valid, they provide a tangibility that is indisputable. Assessment cannot be challenged, and the test is the strictest one'

(Thompson 1967, p. 87). Thus man (in this case the assessor) prefers a determinate, predictable, objectively measurable world. These are the criteria Thompson notes are characteristic of closed-system logic. Yet he rejects this as not being viable for organizations. Why not for individuals?

Some readers may feel that this criticism may be unfair. Thompson is a sociologist and not an economist. They might continue, and I would agree, that Thompson has worked through the basic sociological literature on organizations of the 1940s and 1950s (which had a very strong anti-economic bias) and has arrived at a new way of looking at organizations. It may be that Thompson has ended with views similar to those held by engineering economists and micro-economists several decades ago, but academic fields do go through cycles.

I would agree with this position but wish to argue that those of us working in the field of organizations are necessarily working in a multi-disciplinary field. If we wish to remain within an academic discipline then we should be careful not to focus on generalizations of central concern to other fields. Moreover, our theories are developing to the point where other disciplines cannot be ignored. It may be, as Campbell (1969) suggests, that some fields are best served by the individuals in depth on the theories and data from several academic disciplines as they pertain to the relevant problems.

THE 'APPROPRIATE FIT' OF ORGANIZATIONAL STRUCTURE AND TECHNOLOGY

Finally, let us turn to a basic thesis made by Thompson, namely that there are appropriate fits between task environment and organizational structure and the processes of coordination. For example, technology creates three different types of interdependence among the parts. They are:

Pooled: Each part provides a discrete contribution to the whole and each is supported by the whole, but no direct interaction is required among units.

Sequential: Direct interdependence can be pinpointed between units and the order that interdependence can be specified.

Reciprocal: The outputs of each part becomes inputs for the other. Each unit involved is penetrated and penetrates others (Thompson 1967, pp. 54–5).

Thompson goes on to hypothesize that each type of interdependence has an appropriate method of coordination. They are:

Pooled: Standardization

Sequential: Planning

Reciprocal: Mutual adjustment

By the concept appropriate, Thompson means effectiveness. He would not expect an organization to be effective if its technology required pooled interdependence, yet the method of coordination is mutual adjustment. Conversely a technology characterized by reciprocal interdependence would not be effectively coordinated by standardization.

The difficulty with this scheme can be illustrated when we turn from an appropriate fit or contingency model to a dynamic change model. What would happen if the interdependence changes from pooled to reciprocal? For example a company that existed in a minimally turbulent environment (from an economic view) was suddenly faced with the reality that its major competitor had discovered a way to produce their product at significantly lower costs. The technological environment, for years, had been what Thompson would describe as primarily pooled and secondarily sequential. The method of coordination was, as Thompson would predict, standardization and planning, respectively. But suddenly the organization had to find new ways to cut costs and develop its own new technology. Up to this point little need existed (as Thompson would predict) for reciprocal relationships. However, given the new crisis all the mutual face-to-face influence and cooperation that was humanly possible was necessary. Some did come because of the dire emergency. But the barriers to cooperation, and the attitudes of departmental autonomy, and the expectation to be dependent upon the top, were too strongly entrenched to be overcome easily. The organization began, as predicted by Thompson, to have serious problems.

Although Thompson's theory predicts the consequence, it tends to ignore the variables that could prevent an even worse situation. The face-to-face relationships needed for reciprocal interdependence are very difficult to develop. Moreover, the ones that are associated with pooled and sequential interdependence are difficult to unfreeze (Argyris 1960). In one organization the top management had tried for five years to change the attitudes and behavior about cooperation by standardization and planning, and was still having great difficulties (Argyris 1971a). As we shall see, experiences such as these have led management to question whether the appropriate-fit concept is valid. They have begun to believe that they should aspire to a more organic reciprocal relationship for any technology.

An example of the difficulties one can get into when the appropriate-fit view is used may be found in a recent study by Allen (1970). He studied conglomerates and noted that one way they were able to manage themselves effectively was that the major sub units tended to be self-contained. The only major link to the sub units was the 'one consistent with the requirements of achieving control over total profitability and funds flow' (Allen 1970, p. 3). These findings, Allen points out, are in line with what one would predict from Thompson's theory.

The implicit difficulties with this apparently appropriate relationship surface now that conglomerates are beginning to get into trouble. What is their trouble? Primarily one of funds. What happened? Put simply they milked the sub units and then the entire structure became shaky. In a recent article on what happened as Ling was deposed, one cannot help but wonder if some of the actions that Ling took, in the financial area 'as a one-man show', would have happened if there were relationships of reciprocal and interdependence between Ling and at least a sample of the presidents of the sub units (Sloane 1970). The same questions may be raised in three other cases (*Time* 1970).

The logic of appropriate fit is therefore basically a static model because it hypothesizes effectiveness between the internal and external environments as long as they are congruent and neither changes. In the case above, we have seen that the environment can suddenly change from being benign to becoming turbulent. A mechanistic organization which 'fits' the benign environment (Burns and Stalker 1961, Lawrence and Lorsch 1967) is not necessarily able to change in time toward the organic structure which Thompson states is the appropriate fit for the turbulent environment. Indeed one could argue that the recent difficulties experienced by many of the telephone companies are due to the fact that, although their internal mechanistic systems fitted a benign environment, they also tended to produce rigid, inflexible systems which John Gardner has called organizational dry rot. In his view 'dry rot' has become so serious that he foresees the possibility of a societal breakdown (Gardner 1968). Gardner's diagnoses and conclusions are supported by research of management decision making in thirty different organizations (Argyris 1968). It is concluded that mechanical organizations tend to produce conditions of organizational entropy, to lose ther ability to be innovative, to produce valid information for unimportant problems and invalid information for important ones (Argyris 1968).

Two recent tragic examples of the latter tendency are the apparent massacres by American troops in Vietnam and the near resignations of key Johnson aides over the war. Concerning the former the *New York Times* reports that the 'Army's secret report on the Songmy incident concluded that each successive level of command received a more watered-down account of what had actually occurred in the village' (*New York Times* 1970). As to the latter, Hoopes describes the agony of several top level subordinates who did not agree with the President but did not believe they could communicate their true feelings upward and be heard (Hoopes 1969).

Some top executives have not been blind to the increasing dry rot and its concomittant organizational rigidity. Many of them have begun to think of ways to inhibit the processes that occur, if the research is correct, *regardless of the type of technology*. The dry rot and rigidity may vary in amount. To date however, there is no evidence, that the writer is aware of, indicating that the variance is significantly influenced by the technology. Guest's study of organizational change, for example, shows that remarkable differences were accomplished while the technology remained the same. As Guest (1962) concluded and Perrow supported (1970b, pp. 11–14). the two major factors were leadership style and the administrative posture of the top management.

One possible route is to alter the level of openness, trust, and risk taking at the upper levels. Thus we have the advent of organizational development programs. However, the alternative that is pertinent for this discussion is the use of the matrix system of management in fundamentally pyramidal, mechanistic organizations with a history of pooled and sequential interdependence. Studies have shown that it is extremely difficult for executives to alter their behavior to fit the reciprocal interdependence inherent in a matrix system and manifest the face-to-face mutual influence coordination that is functional in a matrix system. The old values, concepts, and behavior are so powerful that the executives tended to alter the matrix system into a pyramidal one at every feasible opportunity (Argyris 1967).

We conclude that all organizations are continually subject to developing entropy and dry rot, that the best known antidote may be an organic system with reciprocal interdependence and mutual influence. Thus even if one could prove that the external environment of an organization would tend to remain benign, one has to face the fact that mechanistic systems generate internal conditions that lead to an internal environment that makes it increasingly difficult for the organization to remain in valid contact with its external environment and with its internal resources.

Moreover, if this were not the case, mechanistic organizations would find it extremely difficult to become organic when the environment becomes turbulent. Thus recommendations such as Likert's (1967) that the System IV may be valid for all organizations irrespective of their present external environments and technology may be worth serious attention.

SUMMARY

Our analysis suggests:

(1) Although Thompson states that he is studying organizations as wholes, it is more accurate to say that he is studying a part of the organization. No conceptual or operational definition is given for organization 'in the round'.

(2) Although Thompson aspires to present a more realistic integration of the formal and the natural system, the integration actually made favors the closed system, traditional management, economically oriented model which he rejects as incomplete.

(3) The 'variable human' seems to be minimally variable and minimally human. Concerning the former there is no place (in the theory) for individual differences. Concerning the latter, feelings, defenses, needs, self-concept, self-esteems etc. are not included in the theory. The concept of the 'human variable' is only slightly enlarged from economic man and satisfying man. Since, in the theory, the relevant generalizations focus on how the organization induces conformity and nothing about the individual alters the organization, man turns out to be the closed system Thompson so cogently describes as ineffective for existing living systems.

(4) Group dynamic and interpersonal relations are not included. Consequently when multi-variable phenomena are explained (e.g. expansion of financial and economic dimensions of the system) the theory ignores the influence of individual and group factors.

(5) There is a tendency to use economic explanations in ways that do not represent the present state of sophistication of micro-economics.

(6) The basic idea of an appropriate fit between technology, the type of interdependence and organizational structure, is a static concept. It assumes that changes are not going to occur, or, if they are, the organization is able to shift its structure and behavior. The former may be possible, but the latter is questionable without major changes in the variables Thompson chooses to ignore.

(7) There is no apparent way of generating insights about new organizational forms that depend largely or partially on the properties of the individual and the group.

3. CHARLES PERROW

Perrow makes explicit four basic assumptions of his theoretical approach. They are:

(1) Technology is considered the defining characteristic of organizations.

(2) Technology is an independent variable and arrangements to get things done are dependent variables.

(3) Organizations should be studied as 'wholes' rather than deal with specific processes or sub-sections.

(4) Technology is a better basis for comparing organizations than the several schemes that now exist (Perrow 1967, pp. 194–195).

Many of these assumptions are now familiar. Thompson holds strongly, and Blau less so, propositions (1) and (2). Both make the third proposition a central assumption. In the case of the latter we may again raise the question of whether organizations as wholes are something that can be understood without specifying the parts and their interrelationships. What is the conceptual definition of organizations-as-wholes? How is it operationalized? As far as the writer is able to tell none of the authors explicitly define the properties of whole organizations. Nor have they been able to speak causally about the behavior of organizations-as-wholes, without explicitly or implicitly referring to the parts they have chosen to ignore.

ORGANIZATIONAL MAKE-UP AND TECHNOLOGY

The remainder of the assumptions deal with technology, as the defining characteristic, and as the independent variable. We have seen in the analysis of Thompson that technology may or may not be the defining characteristic of organizations. Let us go into more detail on this possibility.

How would Perrow (or Thompson) explain the results of studies into employee morale commitment, and productivity conducted by organizations such as IBM and Sears and Roebuck? These have shown wide variance, even in systems where the technology was constant (Dunnington 1963, Sirota 1963, Klein 1963). Likert's studies of the dysfunctionalities of management Systems I and II show that employee satisfaction and commitment do not tend to vary systematically primarily with technology (1967). The same is true for Argyris (1957, 1960, 1964). Meyer (1968) has described an instrument to measure organizational climate. Included in it are dimensions related to those upon which Perrow focusses attention. For example, constraints resulting from rules, procedures, and policies, responsibility to make decisions, degree of challenge in work etc. In a study of two chemical plants with similar technology he found significant differences in the employees' reports on these factors (1968, pp. 157–8). Moreover he showed even greater differences when two groups, performing 'essentially the same kind of technical and engineering tasks', were studied. He attributed the differences to leadership patterns (1968, pp. 159–60).

The studies quoted in the discussion about Thompson, on the use of matrix organization overlaid on the pyramidal structure, included examples from organizations that were primarily routine or craft industries. Perrow would not expect to find polycentralized, flexible structures in these types of industries. Also there is the interesting history of the Scanlon Plan in organizations which are routine and craft in make-up. Again the matrix committees created by Scanlon placed people from different levels of the hierarchy, gave them equal power, and invested power in the group (Scanlon 1948, Shultz and Cresara 1951 and 1952).

This does not mean that technology is not a key factor. It simply suggests that it is one of several key factors. As Marrow *et al.* have shown, organizational diagnosis and effective changes require a focus on all these factors. What are some of these factors? Elsewhere, I have suggested that there may be at least four defining characteristics of organizations. They are structure and technology, leadership and interpersonal patterns, administrative controls and regulations (budgets, financial statements) and 'human' controls (e.g. much of personnel administration) (Argyris 1957). I have hypothesized further that the potency of these may vary among organizations within the same organization at different points in time) and at different points within the hierarchy. Also, it may be that technology and structure and administrative controls tend to increase their potency as one goes down the hierarchy. Leadership styles and some of the more recent financial computer-based controls, tend to increase their potency as one goes up the hierarchy.

The second difficulty with Perrow's position may be found in his discussion of the relationship between technology and organizational structure (Perrow 1970, pp. 80 ff). His objective is to show that there is a causal relationship between organizational structure and technology. For example, he hypothesizes that certain patterns of discretion, power, coordination, interdependence of groups etc. are caused more by different types of technology than other organizational factors such as interpersonal relationships, leadership and small group dynamics. Why does he discount the role of these factors in his theory? Because 'we must assume that, in the interests of efficiency, organizations wittingly or unwittingly attempt to maximize the congruence between their technology and their structure' (p. 80). But if this assumption is made then the position that technology is the key variable is true by definition. Technology will be the key variable in a theoretical model that assumes that organizations maximize the congruence between technology and structure. As far as I can tell, the circularity of the argument has been ignored by Perrow in his empirical work because he does not study the impact of the variables he believes are unimportant.

Once we are no longer required to accept a tautologically true position, the necessary potency of technology becomes problematical and the possibility that the other factors mentioned above can become potent now becomes more probable. This may help us to understand why Guest's executive (1962) was able to make key organizational changes through leadership style and the top management's willingness to leave him alone (both factors acknowledged by Perrow). It also makes it possible to understand the results reported by Argyris (1965) in three innovative organizations. These organizations fitted in Perrow's quadrants 2 (non-routine) and 3 (engineering). Yet the technical and supervisory levels did *not* report experiencing discretion, power, coordination, and interdependence of groups in Perrow's predicted manner. Interdependence of groups in the flexible, polycentralized organization was low (not high) because it was a basic research laboratory where each unit was left alone. The power and discretion technical staff and supervisors reported they were able to manifest was consistently low. They attributed the cause to the administrative controls and leadership styles of their superiors (all variables that Perrow excluded in his discussion).

These data suggest a third question that must be asked about Perrow's theoretical view, a question that must also be asked about Blau and Thompson. How does one decide if discretion is high or low, if power is high or low? Does one ask a few select senior people (as does Blau) or does one infer it in some objective manner, or does one try to find out how the individuals experience these phenomena? If I understand Perrow correctly, he would not prefer to opt for the third possibility, but in actuality, uses measures of respondents' perceptions. If this interpretation is correct then Perrow has to be careful not to label an aggregate of individual responses as sociological data. What turns an aggregate of individual responses into something other than individual response data is if the theorist can show that the aggregate data leads to a phenomenon at a different level of analysis (which may be shown by making the new level mechanisms or processes that may be involved) (Homans 1964, 1967).

The problem inherent in the question may be illustrated by a paper by Perrow (Perrow IRRA). He begins by telling the reader that size, social function, leadership, history and traditions are far less important than the kind of technology employed (Perrow IRRA, p. 1). We now know that the analysis to which he must be referring may be based on a basic position that is tautological. Then Perrow states, 'But on the shop floor, discretion and power are – should be – *low*' (IRRA, p. 5). Perrow now has switched from making predictions about how power and discretion are to be found to normative statements that they should be found the way he predicts them.

To put this another way, Perrow states that the structures of organizations differ depending upon the requirements of the technology. Woodward takes the same view. A continuous-flow technology has a different structure from a batch technology. Both have stated that an electronic plant (making components) should have a different structure from one making inertial guidance systems components. Why? Because, Perrow replies, organizations have different structures depending upon the kind of search their technology requires (unanalyzable versus analyzable), or the number of exceptions (few or many).

The difficulty with collecting data on these predictions is how does one separate out the influence of leadership styles, administrative controls, norms against risk taking and for conformity etc.? Perrow states that they are unimportant, but does he not need to provide empirical data to show they are? (As we shall see below he is beginning to change his mind.)

A fourth question that may be fruitful to ask is related to Perrow's position on organic systems. 'I have reservations about these labels and some of the normative states in the discussion. For one thing this type of structure is probably only efficient for highly non-routine organizations, and these are few in number, even though they are quite visible and attractive to social scientists who see in them reflections of their academic institutions and values' (Perrow IRRA, p. 5).

Although Perrow presents no data for his gratuitous comment on some social scientists, the difficulty with the statement is his view that academic institutions are to be fitted into his quadrant on non-routine organizations. The validity of this depends upon whom you ask. Senior faculty may agree. Junior faculty, I would be less certain; students, I doubt it. If one understands some of their complaints, it is that too many universities, as they experience them, are in the routine quadrant where the problems are analyzable and few exceptions encouraged. To cite a very old generalization, in understanding people's behavior it is the relative deprivation experienced that is critical. In this sense the students could report *more* deprivation (less discretion, less power, and influence) yet the university technology is not, in Perrow's terms, similar to that of the assembly line. A recent study, for example, presents evidence that students feel manipulated, controlled, and 'dealt with like numbers'. The quantitative scores are as high, if not higher, than those collected for assembly workers (Blauner 1964). Sofer (1970, p. 6) described that half of his executive sample felt 'under-used' and alienated from their work, yet technology is not a key variable for them.

PERROW'S VIEW OF THE NATURE OF MAN

Like Blau, Perrow disavows interest in psychologically based statements, yet he permits them to creep into his analysis. For example, he describes two correctional institutions – one custodial centered (to protect the community from 'dangerous', 'sick' inmates), the other 'treatment' oriented (to help individuals grow and better themselves). He states that the main difference with these organizations is that they conceived the nature of their 'raw' material differently. The custodial institution held, if Perrow will permit, theory *X* view, while the treatment held a theory *Y* view. Then he states 'once a definition is embedded in a program, the opinions of personnel who remain at the institution become congruent with it' (Perrow 1970, p. 34). How is this internalization process to be conceptualized and explained without focussing on psychological processes? This is important because he states that the 'main difference' between the two organizations is the view of the inmates people have internalized.

In another publication, which later became part of the study quoted by Perrow, ample data were given to suggest that many of the inmates fought the custodial view of them (Street 1962). Why did they fight it and the staff (apparently) did not? How can Perrow account for these differences without exploring psychological dimensions?

Permit me to go a little further on this point because I believe it to be an important one; namely that it makes little sense to have only a psychological or sociological view when studying organizations. Both are necessary.

Street (1962), after some preliminary discussion, begins to develop some hypotheses about the inmates' reactions and perceptions under the varying types of institutions. He begins (p. 31) by stating:

(1) Differences in the balance of gratification and deprivation – compared to the custodial institutions, the treatment institutions put much less emphasis upon techniques of degradation, the use of powerful sanction, and denial of impulse gratifications, and place greater stress on providing incentives and objectives and experiences *which are* desired by the inmates. (The italics are mine.)

(2) Differences in patterns of control and authority – compared to the custodial environment, the treatment environment places less importance on surveillance, control over inmate association, proscriptive rules and the protection of social distance between staff and inmates and *lays greater emphasis upon the use of manipulation rather than domination and the attempt to legitimize the organization's authority structure.*

The words in italics are meant to point up the first question that we wish to ask. It is hypothesized (in point 1) that inmates would tend to desire the experience in the treatment institutions. Why should this be so? No data are presented that suggest that the inmates might desire the conditions more typical of the treatment institutions. But, more important in our view, there is nothing in the theory that would suggest the hypothesis. Similarly, it is implied above and made explicit later, that the emphasis on persuasion rather than domination will tend to lead to more 'positive attitudes' and 'cooperation' on the part of the inmates.

Let it be clear that we would tend to agree with the hypotheses. There is no quarrel with them. Nor is there any quarrel with a scholar defining some hypotheses intuitively based on some set of experiences or *a priori* thinking. The objective is to focus on the potential contribution to long-range theory building. Someday it will be necessary, if a theory is to be more fully developed, for these (in our opinion) valid hypotheses to be 'derived' from or somehow related to the theory. This will not be possible, we suggest, until a psychological model of the needs of the inmates is made explicit.

To put this another way, Street has developed in his model of organizations, and Perrow would agree, a list of the demands that each places on the inmates. For example, he writes:

(1) Control is exercised over a greater realm of inmate activities in custodial organizations than in treatment institutions.

(2) The control of inmate behavior in custodial organizations more greatly restricts the inmates' freedom with regard to what previously were minor and personal activities, for example, when to brush one's teeth.

(3) Custodial organizations generally make greater use of practices involving degradation, including rituals of depersonalization at the occasion of the inmate's entry to the organization and continuing with rituals of deference throughout his stay.

(4) In custodial organizations, the staff generally rewards overt conformity to the institutional rules, with little concern for interpsychic or character change. In treatment organizations, the rewarded behavior is more often that which seems to the staff to be indicative of such internal change, a conclusion which may be inferred from the inmate's verbal behavior more than from his overt activities.

(5) Official rules for inmate behavior tends to be more proscriptive in the custodial organizations and more prescriptive in the treatment oriented institutions.

(6) Authority relations in custodial institutions primarily involve

domination and a formal emphasis on obedience, while those in treatment institutions involved informal means of manipulation and persuasion (pp. 29–30).

These organizational 'requirements' are conceptually related to the goals of the organization. All this is eminently sound and valid. Our point is that it is not possible to derive from this theoretical scaffolding the hypotheses, for example (which are stated and later validated), that the custodial institution will have a different impact on the inmates than will the treatment institutions. In order for these hypotheses to be derived from a theoretical framework, one would need to have a model of the needs or predispositions of the inmates.

For example, if we assume theoretically (or for that matter establish empirically) that the inmates aspire toward what Jahoda (1958) calls dimensions of 'positive mental health' we can 'derive' the foregoing hypothesis knowing (as we do) the nature of the organizations (custodial and treatment). Thus, if the inmates aspired toward increased control over their institutional life, independence, and a degree of self-esteem, the custodial institution would be much more frustrating than the treatment institution. The result of frustration would then be shown to lead to the 'negative' attitudes that the author found in the custodial institutions.

The same reasoning seems valid for other hypotheses. For example, 'We expect that the use of extensive and severe measures of control, deprivation, and degradation which substantially limit the available supply of rewards will set the stage for retaliatory and compensatory development of a system for obtaining [other kinds of rewards]' (p. 46).

Why should one expect these consequences? There is little question but that they are probably correct. But such an expectation does not flow from one's sociologically oriented theory. It requires the addition of a theory of personality. For example, one might find highly masochistic, dependent ridden, authority subservient youngsters with a deep sense of psychological failure who might react negatively to the 'positive' treatment milieu and positively to the 'negative' custodial milieu.

Again, 'the inmate group is more likely to take on such political functions and structures, particularly those connected with illicit goods, in the rigorous environment of the custodial institution. In the treatment organization, *because deprivations are low*, and mutual aid less necessary, such an ameliorative system would tend to lose its market' (p. 47).

How is it possible to conceive of a low deprivation without some model of the human personality? How will one judge when a deprivation is a deprivation, not to say whether it is low or not, without some concept of human personality? Moreover, the writer could find nothing in the theory as presented that would lead one to derive the hypothesis just stated.

To put this another way, Street's study and Vinter's and Janowitz's studies actually have implicit in them a model of the needs of the inmates. They implicitly 'correlate' this model with the model of the custodial and the treatment organizations and predict the differential reactions of the inmates. Our attempt here is to suggest that the personality model be made explicit and related to the conceptual apparatus. Indeed, if this were done, it can be shown to lead naturally to a conclusion that Perrow later identifies.

Thus I stated (1964, p. 287) that the organizational goals are an outgrowth from the staff's *concepts about the inmates plus their view of how the inmates are best helped*. Perrow came to the same conclusion in his recent book. But he does not believe that these concepts are *partially* rooted in psychological theory. For example, to state that people have the potential to develop trusting relationships, to grow in 'mature' or 'adult' directions, or that people are unable to trust and to strive toward maturity is to utilize psychological concepts. Here we find an intimate relationship between the psychological and sociological levels. Each institution is composed of staffs that hold different concepts of the needs and potentialities of the inmates. They develop goals and environments (sociological level) that mirror these concepts. Once the goals and environment are created, they feed back to coerce different staff members in the same institution to behave in the same ways.

The point being made is that it may not be useful to insist that the psychological *or* sociological levels of analysis are adequate to understand the total problem. Both are needed (p. 287). This resistance to the inclusion of the psychological dimension leads Perrow to some intellectual gymnastics and contradictions. Concerning the former, he emphasized that the success of the executive in Guest's study was due to his leadership style (a factor which he has not considered major in his theory) and to the fact that the ineffective executive was pressured whereas the effective one was left alone. Perrow then implies that the top management respected the ineffective executive. I doubt this because I have rarely found a management that respected a failing executive and expressed the respect by pressuring him. They usually pressure executives because they do not respect their managerial competence. Even if this interpretation is incorrect, Perrow states that one major cause of the failurc was due to management pressure. If so, why didn't the failing executive ask them to stop pressuring him? May I guess that, given his performance, he knew their answer. On the other hand, the successful executive made and got that request granted *before* he produced any results. I would predict that the reason the request was granted was that they trusted his competence and leadership, and we are back to the individual variable.[1]

SUMMARY

Our analysis suggests:

(1) Although Perrow states that he is studying organizations as wholes, it is more accurate to say that he too is studying a part of the organization. No conceptual operational definition is given for organizations as wholes.

(2) The main thrust that technology is the key variable is based on accepting an assumption that may make it a self-fulfilling prophecy.

(3) The theory makes statements about the relationship between technology and structure which could be reinforced positively or negatively by other relevant variables (e.g. administrative controls, leadership styles etc.). Since these variables are not studied their influence is neither known or understood.

(4) The basic idea of appropriate fit between technology and organizational structure and administrative actions is a static concept. It assumes that changes are not going to occur or, if they are,

[1] A contradiction occurs when Perrow states (1970b, p. 33) that individual personality and styles cannot change organizations, yet in another place he admits McNamara was a key factor in the changes in the Defense Department (p. 26). I should like to mention Perrow's recent paper on departmental power (Perrow 1970a). In this paper he begins to acknowledge 'intermediate variables' which may moderate the impact of technology and exercise of power and discretion. He admits that 'personality factors can have a great deal of influence upon the relations between coordination and subordinate power' (Perrow 1970a, p. 74), and that leadership and organizational history can be important (Perrow 1970a, p. 82).

the organization is able to shift its structure and behavior. Neither is possible without major changes in the variables Perrow chooses to ignore.

(5) Since individuals' perceptions are not considered in the generalizations, the theory makes predictions that may not be true. For example, the theory would predict significantly different behavior and attitudes on the part of workers on assembly lines and students in universities. Yet a theory that includes a psycho-perceptual view could predict the similarities now so clearly observed in our society (e.g. the routineness in life, the constraints of unilateral authority, the pressures to produce).

(6) There is no apparent way of generating insights about new organizational forms that depend largely or partially on the properties of individuals or groups.

4. JOHN GOLDTHORPE AND DAVID LOCKWOOD

The analysis, to date, has emphasized the relevance of psychological data and explanations for the problems that Blau, Thompson and Perrow have conceptualized as being primarily sociological. Effort has been made to avoid the issue of reductionism, i.e. the argument that the psychological is necessarily somehow more basic than the sociological level of analysis. I have repeatedly taken the position that both are necessary, that the results some sociologists obtain are congruent with those stemming from a psychological view, yet the scholars discussed in this paper, to date, either ignore it or maintain it isn't so, that implicit inconsistencies and hypotheses in their work can be made explicit by using concepts from the psychological level, thereby leading to a more internally consistent sociological (if the reader prefers to maintain this distinction) theory.

The same issues will be discussed once more by examining the works of John Goldthorpe and David Lockwood, assisted by Frank Bechofer and Jennifer Platt. The process is repeated for several reasons. Their work represents an important empirical sociological scholarly contribution and it deserves this attention. Unlike the other scholars considered so far, Goldthorpe *et al.* focus more on the sociology of work, and primarily social stratification. The primary attention is on the social activities or behavior of the actors. They are primarily concerned with behavior, which is both oriented toward others and subjectively meaningful to the actor, and we seek to understand this action interpretively in terms of its meaning (i.e. from the actor's point of view) as well as, hopefully, causally in terms of social structural and cultural influences of which actors are not necessarily aware (Goldthorpe, written communication 1971). Thus these writers do not subscribe to the view that social systems can be profitably viewed as autonomous from the individuals in them.

What is the difficulty with such a focus? It is one that some sociologists have been emphasizing. The difficulty does not lie in the focus. Indeed, it is the first one discussed that includes sociological and psychological viewpoints (i.e. social structural variables and the meaning action has to the individual). The case that will be attempted is to show that the exclusion of psychological variables as causal ones places Goldthorpe *et al.* in contradictory positions and makes part of their work incomplete by their own standards and in terms of their own focus. For example, how is it possible to maintain that they do not 'subscribe to the position that the social system can be profitably viewed as autonomous from the individuals in it' and simultaneously seek the causality of individual behavior only in variables that exist in the world outside of the individual? Does not this strategy necessarily imply that individual variables are not potent enough to be needed to understand the causality of individual behavior? If so, then would not this lead to the individual emerging as a passive *tabula rosa* where the social structure and culture determine his behavior? It is as if the individual has little choice and undergoes few important psychological processes as he 'decides' to conform to or accept the demands of the social and cultural world around him. Also, how would one deal with the individual behavior or action that is designed to alter the social structure? Is it possible to conceptualize that as being caused by the same social structure? Also, how can one study the meanings work has for individuals and how these subjective states arise without understanding psychological processes such as cognition and perception?

In seeking to understand the subjective meanings of work Goldthorpe and Lockwood have collected relevant empirical data about the individual. However, our position will be that in looking for causality only 'outside' the individual the resulting *theory* will not be concerned with individuals as central causal variables. Goldthorpe's and Lockwood's view of pinpointing causality 'outside' the individual goes beyond making the individual a part of the system. It tends to create man as a reactive being with few proactive tendencies. The individual becomes a subject, if not a prisoner, of the social structure. This is not the authors' intent for, as we shall see, there is much evidence that they do not see the individual as being completely determined by social structure. Indeed, that is a basic assumption of the social action approach. The hypothesis being suggested is that they will unwittingly not remain consistent with their assumptions when they create a theory whose causal variables remain outside the individual.

Another inconsistency that is an outcome of this approach is related to the authors' views about the concept of psychological needs. Goldthorpe maintains that the concept of psychological needs emphasizes deep and constant needs. He prefers to focus on 'variable wants and expectations determined by social structure and cultural influences rather than relatively constant needs' (Goldthorpe's written communication, 1971). Leaving aside the fact that needs are conceptualized by many psychologists as variable, the inconsistency is that Goldthorpe's view of man does not represent the full variability that is possible because man can have wants and expectations that are deviant from, and inconsistent with, the social culture. Let us explore this point in more detail.

ORIENTATIONS TOWARD WORK

Goldthorpe *et al.* interviewed workers about their wants and expectations. One of their primary findings was that individual workers valued intrinsically satisfying work. For example, the employees who were most satisfied were setters because of opportunity (Goldthorpe *et al.* 1969):

To use their skills:	'Being a setter draws more skill out of you. There's nothing to being an operator; [as a setter] you have to use your brains more...' (p. 13).
To control own work:	'You're left alone – there's only myself on the job. You go along nicely on your own' (p. 13).
To use own initiative:	'I've more opportunity to work on my own initiative and figure things out for myself' (p. 13).
To have variety:	'There's nothing monotonous about it. Most machining is cut up so much that it's all repetition.'

Moreover the craftsmen and setters more frequently gave reasons for their preference to keep their present job (to previous job) by referring to the intrinsic rewards of their jobs (p. 14). The employees who were least satisfied were assemblers, and overwhelmingly preferred jobs that would get them onto jobs which involved work of more variety and challenge and where they would see the product as a whole (p. 15). The authors also note that 'a particularly strong emphasis on the actual nature of their work-tasks is associated *both* with the setter's very high level of job satisfaction and with the assembler's notably low level of satisfaction' (Goldthorpe *et al.* 1969, p. 16).

Finally, where the work tended to provide intrinsic satisfaction, as is the case with the craftsmen, 60% of the total 60 changes suggested had to do with supervision and with tools, equipment and machines. For example:

'One change I'd like to make? The supervision without doubt!'

'I'd like to have the work allocated and then be free to get on with it without immediate supervision.'

'I'd like to see them get rid of the idea that if Harry organized it like that forty years ago, *you've* got to now. I like to use my own initiative.' (Goldthorpe *et al.* 1969, p. 21–2.)

Although the men may have valued work that was intrinsically satisfying, most did not report that they were actively seeking such work. Most reported, in several different ways, that they were seeking high pay, job security, adequate benefits etc. from their work. Moreover, a sub-sample actually left intrinsically satisfying work in order to go to jobs that paid more and had greater security. These predominant wants or expectations for money and job security the authors defined as representing an instrumental orientation. Their argument is '... among the men we studied a particular *orientation* [italics theirs] to work – one of a markedly instrumental kind – is predominant' (Goldthorpe *et al.* 1969, p. 1). In a later book, they write, '... the current orientation of these men toward their work was a decidedly *instrumental* [italics theirs] one' (Goldthorpe *et al.* 1969, p. 56).

Many may be conceptualized as manifesting work orientations. One of these is an orientation toward work that is intrinsically satisfying the other an orientation that conceives of work as an instrumental activity. If one focusses on what affluent workers tend to choose – not necessarily value – the majority experience and choose work as an instrumental activity. What is more the workers who do so are not sufficiently dissatisfied to be any less effective in their work.

EXPLAINING THE INSTRUMENTAL ORIENTATION

Why do many affluent workers manifest an instrumental orientation? The researchers, following their theory, looked in the sociocultural context for answers to this question and found quite a few. The affluent worker reported closer contact with his family and greater need to obtain intrinsic satisfaction with them. Therefore he wanted to own his home (and get away from living with either set of parents), he wanted to provide his family with a certain minimal degree of security; he wanted a better life, in the sense of being able to buy more of the consumer products available and traditionally aspired to by the middle classes. A sub-set of the affluent workers may have chosen the instrumental orientation because they had become downwardly mobile, from their middle class family background, and they wanted to maintain the life they knew when they were younger. Moreover, the instrumental attitude fitted with the time of life when the breadwinner was recently married and looked forward to raising his family.

Note: Working man has now become predominantly instrumental man; the primary causes for the instrumental orientation lie outside the individual, and intrinsic orientation is devalued. Thus:

> Our major aim has been to indicate a certain homogeneity in our sample of affluent workers in terms of their orientation to work and associated attitudes and behavior in the work situation. Variations in these respects have been observed from one occupational group to another. But, we have argued, these can be best understood as variations on, or sometimes as deviations from, a central tendency, that of regarding work *in a predominantly instrumental way*. This instrumental orientation... is one which, to some significant degree, extends across occupational divisions reflecting differences in skill and status and which would appear to override perhaps yet more decisively the possible effects upon industrial attitudes and behavior of different production technologies (Goldthorpe *et al.* 1968, p. 144).

The instrumental orientation may be so coercive that it overrides the powerful effects attributed to the different production technologies by men like Thompson and Perrow. The work factors inside the organization and on the job become less potent.

Yet the same authors state: '... it was this immediate relationship between men and their jobs which was the aspect of their work most capable of producing either some feeling of personal fulfillment or, on the other hand, some clear sense of deprivation (Goldthorpe *et al.* 1968, p. 16), and 'We agree with those who insist upon the fundamental importance of the content of work-tasks to job satisfaction and go clearly against the idea that factory workers are simply "happy robots"' (Goldthorpe *et al.* 1968, p. 16).

How did the authors go from a position that the work-tasks or the on-the-job variables are critical ones, to a position that the instrumental orientation overrides these factors? I should like to suggest that the answer lies in their excluding certain individual level variables.

IS THE INTRINSIC ORIENTATION DEVALUED?

Let us begin by reminding the reader that the data that led to the conclusion that the instrumental work orientation was predominant were obtained, *at the same time*, and from the same workers, who spoke of the importance of instrinsically satisfying work. This means that the workers spoke of the importance of intrinsic work satisfactions while, in the Goldthorpe *et al.* sense, their primary work orientation was an instrumental one. However prepotent the instrumental work orientation may have been, it was not so prepotent that it suppressed the attraction that intrinsic work had for the respondents.

But, Goldthorpe *et al.* would respond, we have never said that workers do not value intrinsically satisfying work. Indeed, our own data were cited above pointing to the desire for work that was intrinsically satisfying. Our position is that we focus on what men choose. They choose instrumental work; in many cases they leave work that is intrinsically satisfying and go toward work that has little intrinsic satisfaction but pays much more money and has more job security.

The writer would agree with Goldthorpe *et al.* as far as empirical data are concerned. What Goldthorpe *et al.* do not seem to focus on, *in their theory*, are (1) the processes by which the workers perceived, accepted and internalized the instrumental attitudes, (2) the processes that they experienced as individuals, to select the instrumental over the intrinsic orientation, and (3) the psychological mechanisms of, and the consequences for, a human being who has little choice but to enter work that is not intrinsically satisfying.

Perhaps the issue may be clarified by asking how the social and cultural variables identified by Goldthorpe *et al.* explain the following phenomena which were also found to exist among the same affluent workers and at the same time.

Psychological and physical stresses among employees

> ... among our affluent workers generally, the experience of monotony of unabsorbing work and of an excessive pace of work were all apparent sources of deprivation and of job dissatisfaction; and, second, that at least with some groups in the sample, such experience would seem to be more than usually widespread, in the light of more intensive studies of factory employees. In other words, it could be said that, among our affluent workers, the performance of work tasks was accomplished by various and in some groups fairly generalized, psychological or physical stresses (Goldthrope *et al.* 1968, pp. 19 and 20).

The meaning of work as 'labor'

> Over all, therefore, it could not be claimed that our affluent workers derived any very high degree of satisfaction immediately from the work-tasks and roles which they performed.
>
> ... with the majority of the semi-skilled men, at least, their work was largely experienced and regarded as an expenditure of effort made with the aim and expectation of extrinsic rather than intrinsic returns: in other words, the meaning which was given to work was essentially that of *labor* (Goldthorpe *et al.* 1968, p. 25).

The dilemma of choosing instrumental over intrinsic work orientations

> ... we would suggest, a fairly distinctive, and widely felt dilemma of working-class occupational life; the dilemma, that is, of having to *choose between* [italics theirs] work which offers variety, scope for initiative and relative autonomy, and

work which, for any skill level, affords the highest going rate of economic return. The men who made up our critical case had opted for this latter alternative . . . [in effect they chose consciously] to *devalue* [the intrinsic aspects of work] (Goldthorpe *et al.* 1969, p. 64).

How can individuals who have (a) selected the instrumental orientation, (b) have made it prepotent, and (c) have devalued the intrinsic orientation, also experience 'fairly generalized psychological or physical stresses', and develop a meaning of work as 'labor', and experience 'a fairly widely felt dilemma of working-class occupational life'? Does not this mean that the intrinsic orientation is, *psychologically*, a very crucial one but in social, action terms, it probably cannot be a realistic choice? Most jobs that are available to the worker do not have significantly large components of intrinsic work components. Moreover, the workers, due to the available level of wages and security, may be locked into maintaining their physiological and security needs. As Maslow has suggested, under these conditions, people would not be expected to seek work to fulfill self-actualizing needs (Maslow 1954).

It may be valid to suggest that because Goldthorpe *et al.* omitted the psychological dimensions from their theory, they had to ignore seeking explanations for the feelings that individuals have when they are 'forced' to choose a work world where intrinsic work is lacking and where the only major type of needs that can be satisfied are instrumental ones. One would have to focus on individual internal conflict processes to explain the mechanisms of psychological stresses; on psychological cognitive processes to understand the mechanisms by which work becomes essentially labor; on psychological decision processes by which dilemmas are experienced and overcome.

Man, as Goldthorpe *et al.* describe him, empirically, is more complicated therefore than what the concept of instrumental work orientation includes. The affluent workers may actively value both orientations, for different reasons, and know that, given the design of the present work world, there is little probability of satisfying the intrinsic orientation. Thus they go through certain psychological processes to suppress their expectancy for intrinsic satisfaction while at work and focus on obtaining all the instrumental rewards they can get. Thus, it is probably true, as Goldthorpe *et al.*

state, that workers came to their present employment primarily attracted by the extrinsic and economic returns. But those kinds of findings cannot be adequately explained by the concept of instrumental orientation for two reasons. First, the explanation is circular. The concept of instrumental orientation was inferred from the workers' responses that they were seeking extrinsic and economic rewards.

More importantly perhaps, the concept of instrumental work orientation cannot, by itself, explain Goldthorpe *et al.*'s conclusion that affluent workers were attracted to extrinsic and economic rewards in *compensation for* [italics theirs] the lack of intrinsic satisfactions at work. If an employee were genuinely primarily instrumentally oriented, why would he seek compensation for the lack of intrinsic satisfactions? Also, if the instrumental work orientation were prepotent then how can Goldthorpe *et al.* explain the degree of dissatisfaction revealed by the craftsmen by the 'fact that these men have expectations... which take for granted fairly high economic returns *and* [italics mine] which are also concerned with the degree to which the individual is allowed to exercise his skills in an autonomous way'? (Goldthorpe *et al.* 1968, p. 25).

A PSYCHO-SOCIOLOGICAL THEORY WHICH WOULD EXPLAIN THE GOLDTHORPE ET AL. FINDINGS

I should like to describe a theoretical framework which includes the psychological dimensions excluded by Goldthorpe *et al.* and supports their views but provides them (1) with an *a priori* prediction of the instrumental attitude, (2) a more parsimonious explanation for some of their other findings (as well as the findings of some other sociologists working in this area), and (3) a prediction that the intrinsic orientation can be maintained while the instrumental attitude influences behavior (such as remaining or leaving the organization).

By exploring the descriptive research literature in developmental psychology, it was inferred that the behavior of infants in the Christian-Judaic world could be *described* as being dependent upon, and submissive to, parents (or other significant adults) and that they manifested few abilities. Adults were *described* as behaving in ways that suggested they sought to minimize dependence, to gain control over their immediate world, to develop many abilities

(Argyris 1957). These and other qualities were developed into dimensions upon which any individual could be placed and profile could be developed.

Next, the question was asked, what would happen if people aspired toward the adult ends of the continua and were placed in assembly line work? Knowing the conditions that such work offered, the answer came that individuals would experience frustration, psychological failure, short-time perspective. The next question was how do people adapt to these states of affairs? The answer included behavior-patterns that were being documented under the concept of informal activities plus absenteeism, turnover and unionization.

Another major prediction was that if people decided to accept this state of affairs, they would do so because it fulfilled some need. One such need was to get out of the state of affairs and minimize the necessity to continue this life outside of work. Money and benefits was one critical way to assure this need. Moreover, these economic rewards helped to guarantee the fulfillment of the basic psychological needs of subsistence and security (Maslow 1954). Finally, accepting money as a pay-off for frustration etc. fitted with the economic logics of the organization.

However, it was also predicted that in order to make this psychological withdrawal from work and yet to continue to work physically, in spite of the reality that the work continued to be impoverished, the employees, in order to live with themselves, must somehow devalue *in the work situation* the importance of human factors (such as self-esteem) and value material factors (such as money). Thus one arrives at the notion of market-orientation stated by Fromm (1955), or Goldthorpe's and Lockwood's view of instrumental attitudes. Given this view, it was predicted that:

(1) Employees would tend to place increasing emphasis on monetary rewards as a pay-off.

(2) The relationship between work-effort and economic rewards would tend to decrease. Wages will become more rewards for the dissatisfying impoverished work world in which the worker was placed and less as rewards for productivity.

(3) Employees would tend to suppress (not repress) their needs to intrinsic satisfaction, and to use their abilities to have greater control. Thus even if affluent, they would be able to identify and discuss, and value intrinsic satisfactions. They simply will not expect to

obtain such satisfactions at work. They would go along with the frustration as long as they were paid off (Argyris 1957).

These predictions fit the data presented at the outset. They also fit the conclusions stated by Goldthorpe *et al.* For example:

> (1) From the findings that we have reviewed, it is therefore fairly apparent that for many of the affluent workers we studied, affluence had been achieved only at a price: that of accepting work which affords little in the way of intrinsic rewards . . . Indeed one could say that many of these men have gained their 'middle-class' incomes and standards of living through taking and holding jobs which offer higher pay than do most types of manual work *because* [italics theirs] of the stresses and deprivations they impose (1968, p. 58).
>
> (2) Their concentration on gaining, as wage workers, a steadily increasing 'take' from their firms, rather than an occupational advance within it, underlies the extent to which their relationship with their employer is purely a *market or contractual one* [italics mine], containing few of the important moral elements that figure . . . in the employment relationship of bureaucratic personnel: for instance the obligation to put these abilities fully and faithfully at the service of the organization (Goldthorpe *et al.* 1968, pp. 80–1).

In one study, it was noted that the definition of a good supervisor was one 'who let you alone', 'who keeps to himself' (Argyris 1960), a finding which Goldthorpe *et al.* confirm (1968, p. 66). One can explain the preference for such leadership by evoking the concept of instrumental attitude and the potency of economics. However, it is difficult to see how the concepts will explain the attitudes of craftsmen, indicated above, that one reason they preferred to be left alone was to be able to use their initiative to have some control over their immediate work. This finding is explainable in terms of our theory.

To state this another way, in addition to the Goldthorpe *et al.* explanation being circular, they offer no explanation and therefore no *a priori* prediction why workers develop an instrumental attitude *or* how they can manifest genuine value for self-expression on the job while holding instrumental attitudes.

Still another problem inherent in the framework used by Goldthorpe *et al.* may be illustrated by their findings regarding the outside activities of the affluent worker. Some sociologists have assumed that outside work activities are dictated largely by the values and norms of the social class in which one belongs. If workers became affluent and, economically and educationally, began to reach middle-class status, would they also take on the sociability patterns of the middle class?

Goldthorpe *et al.* found that they did not adopt middle class values. They 'devoted most of their time to home and family life rather than to sociability of any more widely based kind' (p. 103). Why was this the case? Goldthorpe *et al.* suggest two reasons. First the long-standing working class norms of sociability are brought into the new economic and social conditions (p. 103). Second, they introduce into their explanation 'a more radical sense' of status dissent. They suggest that these employees 'dissent from the middle-class conception of the status hierarchy, from the values of 'status striving' and in particular from the idea that white collar jobs confer upon their occupants any degree of social or moral superiority that might make such persons fit objects for the manual worker's deference and emulation' (Goldthorpe 1969, pp. 114–15).

Our explanation would be more parsimonious since we would not have to introduce a new concept (status dissenters). Our view would be that the 'keeping to one's self and family' sociability patterns may be related to the aloneness and keeping to one's self that the individual learns inside the plant. A market-oriented employee who has suppressed many human values and learned to emphasize material values may have also learned that the world, especially inside the plant, is not very sympathetic and 'making a buck' is what really counts. Under those conditions perhaps the best assurance of comfort and genuineness is in his family relationships. Moreover, given a de-emphasis on human values, one can predict that the individual will not tend to seek to enlarge his interpersonal and social contacts. Most importantly, since nothing *on the job* has changed for the worker, he would continue to experience the same psychologically impoverished world he would have if he were not affluent, including seeking no increase in opportunity to advance himself (Goldthorpe *et al.* 1968 agree, see pp. 76–84). Thus why should the individual seek more work challenges to use more of his abilities, and to aspire higher (middle class value)? More importantly why should he accept 'middle class superiority' over the kind of human being he *is* and the kind of human existence he *lives*?

The thrust of the argument to date is that the individual and sociological approaches have a legitimate existence. However, for the problems discussed by sociologists like Goldthorpe and Lockwood, it would be scientifically more comprehensive and parsimonious if the individual level were given a more powerful role. But now I should like to go further and hypothesize that the approach that travels from the 'inside' (of the organization) toward the outside (and returns) can be more comprehensive than the approach that begins by looking at the environment and then travels into the organization. The factors inside the organization can 'spill over' and influence life satisfactions outside of the organization (Kornhauser 1965, Iris and Barrett 1970).

This hypothesis is based upon the assumption that if these two approaches were studied systematically, the approach that focussed first on the individual and his job requirements would be found to account for more of the non-random variance related to these issues, than the approach that began by looking at social class or any other political-economic explanation. Recently Kohn (1969) and Kohn and Schooler (1969) who have worked with the latter approach, reported data related to this hypothesis. The data came from three studies. The first was a national sample of 3,101 men that was representative of all men employed. The second was a study of 520 mothers and 341 fathers in Italy. The third was 339 mothers and 82 fathers in Washington D.C. Our focus will be primarily on the study of the national sample (Kohn and Schooler 1969). Their findings may be organized in the following outline form:

(1) There is a linear relationship between values on conformity to externally imposed rules versus self-direction from the highest to the lowest socio-economic class. The relationship is essentially the same for whatever age and size of family (p. 664).

(2) Consonant with greater valuation of self-direction, men of higher class were found to take extrinsic aspects of jobs (pay and security) for granted and focus on opportunities jobs offer for self-expression and individual accomplishment.

The higher the men's social class, the more importance they attach to how interesting the work is, the amount of freedom, the opportunity to use their abilities, and the chance to help people. The lower their class position, the more importance they attach to pay, fringe benefits, hours of work etc. (p. 666).

(3) The class relationships are predominantly linear, with virtually

no significant curvilinear or higher order relationships and no sharp breaks. It is profitable to think of a continuous hierarchy of positions, not of discrete social classes (p. 669).

So far these results are consistent with the work of the authors cited in this paper. The last finding especially supports Goldthorpe's questioning of the existence of discrete social classes.

(4) Education and occupational position are each related, independently of the other, to almost all aspects of values and orientation and these relationships are essentially additive. Education and occupational position are important in understanding:

(a) self-direction versus conformity to externally imposed rules,

(b) valuing intrinsic or extrinsic aspects of work, and less so

(c) self-confidence and self-deprecation (p. 669).

(5) Income and class identification are *not* very important for explaining the relationships of class to 4 (a), (b) and (c) (p. 669). The authors' data begin to question Goldthorpe's hypothesis of the primacy of economic motives but support his view of the lack of potency of class identification as an explanatory concept.

Why is this so? What are the most potent variables influencing these relationships? After a careful statistical analysis of their data, the authors conclude that 'only those conditions that vary continuously with education and with occupational position can be of great relevance to understanding such factors' as those in 4 (a), (b) and (c).

Although educational experience is a potent variable, occupational position is more potent (p. 675). The aspect of occupational conditions that is most potent is occupational self-direction (pp. 674–5).

If occupational position is crucial and if, within that, self-direction permitted on the job is most important, and if economic and class identification are not significantly related to self-direction, then the direction to look for the potent variables is inside the organization.

For example, Kohn and Schooler show that: (a) closeness of supervision is significantly related to occupational self-direction; (b) the work is also critical. Work with data or with people is more likely to require initiative and thought and judgment than is work with things. Work that is more complex and less routine is related to occupational self-direction.

Thus we arrive at the point where the key factors identified with occupational position are those, *on the job*, that, on the one hand, are related to providing opportunities for greater control over one's work, less dependence upon others, especially supervision, and more use of one's abilities and, on the other hand, those factors, *on the job*, that provide little opportunity for self-control, and for use of one's abilities.[1] These two sets of factors are congruent with the conditions Argyris showed represented some of the key dimensions along which infancy and adulthood have been studied by personality researchers. The Goldthorpe view of the primacy of economic motives and the Lockwood view of a new mode of social consciousness are neither confirmed by their data nor are they necessary if one uses our theory. The Goldthorpe *et al.* findings can be explained by the Kohn and Schooler findings as fitted into the Argyris model as follows. The primacy of instrumental attitudes may be caused by jobs that have little intrinsic pay-off and little opportunity for self-direction and the use of one's abilities. Lockwood's view that workers are less focussed on power as the crucial factor in order to influence society, is explained by the Kohn and Schooler data that the lower the class of the worker, the greater their conformity to external societal norms, the more conservative, the more willing to accept rules. Hewitt also concludes that the lower strata 'stress unquestioning adherence to rules' (1970, p. 62). Finally, the parents tend to inculcate their children with these values so that they become carriers for these values.

One approach is also helpful in explaining related research in a more parsimonious manner. For example, Perlin reports that 'alienation [is] most intensive under conditions of great [positional] disparity' (Perlin 1962, p. 316). Wide positional disparity, he continues, restricts reciprocity, decreases spontaneity, and increases the unilaterial influence along lines of formal authority (p. 317). These findings may be translated into our framework as follows. Any variable (including positional disparity) that decreases the subordinates' control and increases his dependency tends to increase the feelings of alienation. However, translating one generalization to another is not adequate incentive for selecting from a choice of frameworks. The advantage of ours, it is suggested, is that it

[1] It may also be that the relationships between self-direction and organizational experiences are partially explained by early life experiences and subsequent occupational choice. If so, then the impoverished work experiences may interact with early life experiences and occupational choice to produce the results described above.

explains other Perlin findings without adding new concepts or generating explanations that may be totally or largely tautological (depending on the measures). For example, Perlin notes that the findings stated above do not hold for some employees. He posits that there are people who have attitudes of 'status obeisance'. These people revere status and would not therefore be alienated by being dependent, submissive etc. Our view does not require any new concepts. I would hypothesize that the individuals who may need to be dependent and submissive will not feel a sense of alienation.

Is it not possible that some people may revere status and not be dependent oriented? The early work on the authoritarian personality suggested that dependence and reverence to authority were significantly positively correlated (Sanford *et al.* 1956). However, our theory would permit a differentiation to be made between reverence for authority and the needs to be dependent and submissive etc. Perlin's framework, as presently constituted, would not make this differentiation. It would require a model of the individual personality which is lacking.

The same problem exists with Blauner's work although he acknowledges that his framework assumes a model of man that he never makes explicit (Blauner 1964, p. 15). Although Blauner recognizes this important omission, Smelser and Davis (1969), when they discuss his work, do not. They quote extensively findings that cannot be explained without the psychological dimension. The danger in their omission of this possibility may be made evident when we realize that their book is an example of how sociology can be of help in understanding our societal problems and changing them. I am suggesting that such an 'understanding' is incomplete and would predict that change would not be possible without correcting this omission.

For example, why do they say, 'as expected the auto workers were highest on alienation scores and printers lowest?' They would reply that 'the auto worker has little control over his conditions of work, little relief from monotony etc.; by contrast the printer has greater control of his work, less monotony etc.' (Smelser and Davis 1969, p. 14). No one disagrees with the findings about the nature of the work. The problem arises when one attempts to predict what is the impact of these conditions upon individuals and a prediction about alienation attempts to do just this. Then one needs to know something about the meaning of work for the employee, and the way he orders his needs. The latter data are non-existent in the Blauner study; they are assumed.

Again the difficulty with the Blauner framework would be to explain some of the data from Goldthorpe *et al.* where they report less concern in some of Blauner's criteria for alienation, namely powerlessness and helplessness. Also how would Blauner explain that the degree of 'alienation' or estrangement from work in high skill and low skill employees was about the same in two organizations with similar technology (Argyris 1960), without knowing something about the needs of the employees and their modes of adaptation to work?

Recently Silverman (1970) has proposed an action frame of reference. Such a frame of reference focusses explicitly on the meaning that any given situation has for a given actor. He believes that sociology should be concerned with action which arises out of meanings which define social reality. Meanings are given to men by their society. Through their interactions, men also modify, change, and transform social meanings.

Silverman's stated position is consonant with the one suggested in this analysis. It focusses on the individual and structural (cultural) factors. However, when Silverman describes how one goes about empirically understanding individual meanings he seems to reject his own axioms. He opts for an approach that is clearly one-sided. For example, he states that explanations, 'are in terms of ideal-typical actors whom we take to be pursuing certain ends by choosing appropriate means on the basis of a subjective definition of the situation'. He quotes Shultz approvingly that to understand meanings it is sufficient to find typical motives of typical actors which explain the act as a typical one arising out of a typical situation (Shultz and Cresara 1951, p. 139).

To the writer's knowledge, Silverman does not explain how a 'typical motive' is identified; how a 'typical actor' is identified. Nor does he seem aware of the apparent inconsistency between such explanatory concepts and his insistence that explanation should be based upon understanding the meaning of reality for any given actor. Nowhere are we told how to deal empirically with actors who are not 'typical'. Do not the concepts of typical motive and typical actor ignore individual differences, a phenomenon that Silverman argues any theory should respect? Moreover, is it not possible that in some cases it will be the atypical actor holding atypical motives who may be crucial in questioning the system and bringing about change? Also, how does Silverman, who rejects constructs that are created by the researchers (to infer what is in the life space of the individual), create a 'typical motive' or a 'typical actor' without doing the very type of conceptualizing that he rejects?

As Goodman has pointed out, Silverman has placed himself in an inconsistent position (1971, pp. 132–4). Goodman writes, 'Instead of focussing on an individual-based sociology which is the logical outcome of his argument, he falls back upon the "ideal-typical" organizational member. He builds the same sort of observer-based construct which he denies to other theorists, that is, one which does not have meaning in the life space of the organizational actor.'

In addition to the apparent inconsistency, Silverman leaves several critical methodological questions unanswered. The first is, how does one infer meanings, be they typical or not? What precisely does the scholar do when he is in an organization? Does he interview? Observe? Use questionnaires? Moreover, how can he develop instruments that ignore human behavior? Is it not necessary, if one is to obtain the meanings as held by individuals, to make some inferences from their behavior (in addition to asking them questions by one form or other)? If not, how would Silverman cope with such findings that suggest that many individuals are not aware of the large and consistent discrepancy between how they perceive the meaning that their behavior has for others and what it actually does mean to the other? (Argyris 1968). Also, how does action 'arise out of meanings which define social reality'? How are 'meanings given to man by their society'? How do men 'through their interactions, modify, change, and transform social meanings'?

The writer is not suggesting that Silverman should have provided full-blown answers to these most difficult and basic questions. I am suggesting, however, that Silverman might find it useful to explore the literature which has dealt with these questions, and which has contributed much more empirical research than any other. Silverman does not seem to have felt it necessary to study, for example, the works of cognitive social psychologists such as Kurt Lewin and Fritz Heider, nor psychological ecologists such as Roger Barker and Herbert Wright. Even a rapid examination of this literature would have unearthed the conclusion reached by most of them, namely that meanings cannot be empirically identified by ignoring behavior.

Lewin, in his discussions of life space, and Heider, in his discussions of how people develop meanings for themselves (explored in attribution theory), have shown how understanding begins (not ends) by observing human behavior. Nor does Silverman seem to be concerned with the literature on perceptual social psychology which focusses on how people perceive reality and develop meanings. Perhaps Silverman has explored this literature and found it wanting. That would be important to know.

Some readers may suggest that Silverman need not explore this literature because he is taking a sociological perspective. I question this position. A scholar should be required to examine any serious literature that is directly relevant to his axioms and propositions. Anyone stating as an axiom that individual psychological meanings can be studied without focussing on behavior is making a critical assumption that requires careful documentation precisely because we are asked to accept it as a basic given.

A third methodological issue that suffers from an exploration of the relevant literature is the one related to the use of the concept of need to understand and explain the actor's meanings. The concept of need is for Silverman 'the crux of the difference between the sociological perspective and the self-actualizing school of psychology' (p. 86). Silverman suggests that those interested in self-actualization conceptualize all needs as basic, unchangeable, and consistent throughout all situations. Thus an individual is hypothesized to be self-actualizing in all situations, including those where it may not be possible. Moreover, he suggests that these same scholars view man as so committed to self-actualization that they cannot conceive man as capable of depotentizing his need for self-actualization in the work situation. For example, Silverman asks if there are not workers who do not aspire to actualize themselves, to enhance their self-esteem, or to feel essential? May not workers, for instance, actually desire jobs that offer little opportunity for initiative and responsibility? (p. 87).

The answer is, as we have pointed out in the discussion of Goldthorpe and Lockwood, that such 'needs' are perfectly possible; indeed one can have a theory about human behavior in which the concept of need is central and make specific predictions about individual behavior and organizational activities under these conditions.

Why does this apparent misunderstanding arise? This question perplexes the writer because the literature on the concept of psychological needs is so voluminous. The questions and doubts raised by Silverman about the concept of needs has been raised for at least two decades. For example, there is the pioneering discussions by Angyal (1941), Hall and Lindzey (1957), Kluckhohn and Murray (1949), and Lewin (1935). Reading such materials, it is possible to develop the following generalizations about the concept of need.

(1) The concept of need was useful in helping to understand the movement or direction of human behavior.

(2) The concept of need was most effective when related to goals in the environment.

(3) Needs existed at several different levels. Some needs were peripheral, some inner, and some more central. The same was true for goals.

(4) Human beings could develop needs within and between each level that ranged from being consonant with each other to being antagonistic with each other.

(5) In order to understand human behavior it was important to understand *all* the different levels of needs. There was little sense in saying that one level of need was more important than another for the explanation of human behavior. Each level of needs was most effective for explaining behavior at that level. This is the meaning of Kluckhohn's and Murray's famous statement that every man is in certain respects: (a) like all other men; (b) like some other men; (c) like no other man (Kluckhohn and Murray 1949, p. 35).

Thus, one can use the concept of need and not be required to reject the sociological framework recommended by Silverman. The important point is to select the level of need that is most appropriate for the behavior in question. It always appeared invalid to the writer, for scholars to identify one set of needs with a particular research group as if they excluded the needs that they were not studying. For example, for Silverman to state that Roethlesberger and his group saw man's primary motivating force as his 'need' to interact with, and to be accepted by, his fellows (p. 78), is to greatly oversimplify their views. To be sure, the original Hawthorne researchers focussed *initially* on needs of interrelatedness because their early studies uncovered the importance of these needs. But they continued by exploring such needs as success, failure, competence and power. Similarly, Maslow, as a hard-headed experimentalist and later as a clinician, was aware that not all people strove to actualize themselves. Indeed, he was very careful to point out that relatively few people were actualizers. His concept of deficiency orientation was operationally defined to include many needs that had little to do with growth and self-actualizations as he used the concept. Moreover, Maslow always accepted the notion that different levels of needs were needed to understand human behavior. Scientists of personality as indicated by the references listed above, have, for at least two decades, seen man as 'complex man' (the concept of man which Silverman seems to accept as a relatively new one and one that is most valid for understanding human behavior).

Complex man can manifest inner, central, and peripheral needs. Scholars such as Maslow, Lewin, Rogers, Fromm, Angyal (to mention but a few) have focussed on such needs as self-esteem, competence, essentiality, and self-actualization because they find these needs helpful in understanding certain human behavior. Such needs help them to explain more peripheral, more transitory, more situationally-based needs. But, in doing so, they do not deny the relevance of these more peripheral needs. It is possible to make perfectly good explanations (to predict and control behavior) by focussing on such peripheral needs. What makes some needs more basic (less situation-based) is that they seem to be valued by individuals and they seem to maintain their potency even if their expression, in a given situation, is not possible. For example, as pointed out in the analysis of the Goldthorpe and Lockwood work, although the instrumental orientations (which would be more situationally-based needs) were being actively pursued by workers, these same workers still valued highly the intrinsic needs (which would be less situation-based, for example, would be viewed by the workers as desirable to express in their homes, work, and recreation).

Silverman apparently doubts the hypothesis suggested by the writer that if needs such as competence and self-esteem are not being actively pursued by the workers it is because they have come to realize that the probability for their expression in the work situations is not very high (1970, p. 87). The writer concluded that if they are not actively pursued they may still be potent but understandably suppressed. Silverman quotes the writer accurately as stating that systematic tests that directly test the hypothesis of suppression were not available. Silverman fails to continue quoting from the same discussion the four studies cited which indirectly test this hypothesis. Nor does he cite the studies of a national sample (Argyris 1962, p. 54) and of automobile workers (pp. 55 and 56) in which evidence is presented that lower level employees value self-actualization-type needs as much as top executives and managers. All these studies provide evidence that is much more direct than Ingham's (1967) or Gouldner's (1954) studies that Silverman uses as his major illustration of his position.

It is perfectly consistent to believe that man is capable of valuing self-esteem, competence, etc. and also to view man as seeking fulfillment of other needs in the organizational world. For example, the writer has conducted several studies where the focus was on 'predispositions' which were defined as tendencies to act in a particular manner under specific conditions (Argyris 1954, 1956, and 1960, pp. 65–6). Predispositions were defined as being neither 'in' the individual nor 'in' the environment. They were interactional concepts. The writer stated, 'It should be made clear that a predisposition is *not assumed* to be as the need or need systems postulated by many psychologists. Their concepts usually refer to phenomena that are more genotypic than that to which we refer' (Argyris 1960, pp. 65–6). If one examines the detailed descriptions of the way these predispositions were inferred and quantified, they represented, I believe, a viable and valid methodology for achieving what Silverman recommends. The personalizing and socializing scores represent an attempt to show how the organization socializes the individual, and the personalizing scores, how the individual modifies the organization. In these studies not only was an individual differences analysis shown to be possible (without having to create ideal-typical constructs), but individual and group behavior of subjective and objective kinds was predicted with respectable accuracy.

A fourth set of methodological problems not, as yet, resolved are those involved with organizational change. After criticizing many different scholars, Silverman concludes that, 'a great deal of organizational analysis has tended to concentrate on the external sources of change' (p. 152). This is hardly surprising, according to Silverman, because many of these organizational theorists often assume that organizations have an inherent strain towards internal equilibrium. The great merit of the action approach is to be able to explain how changes arises out of the interaction of the actors.

It is not clear who Silverman had in mind when he refers to 'a great deal of organizational' research that assumes organizations manifest an inherent strain towards internal equilibrium. The writer is part of such a group of researchers. Yet this view has never seemed to be a barrier to explain change out of the interaction of the actors. This is a fundamental building block of his organizational change programs (Argyris 1962, 1965, 1970 and 1971). This point is being made less with the intention of pointing out Silverman's omissions and much more with the purpose of showing that it does not follow, as Silverman states, that those who assume a tendency toward internal equilibrium will not be able to focus on change through the interaction of the actors.

A fifth methodological issue identified by Silverman, as resolved appropriately by the action approach, is related to descriptive versus prescriptive research. In several places in the book, Silverman defines the role of the sociologist as descriptive. Apparently the sociologist should shun developing theory from which one can derive and test prescriptive generalizations. Although the writer would agree with Silverman when he condemns too early or too incomplete prescriptive efforts, it has been a central position of this analysis that a publically verifiable valid (descriptive) theory of organizations will require certain kinds of empirical tests that cannot be executed without some prescriptive or normative assumptions. As far as the writer could ascertain, Silverman ignores this possibility and creates a point of view where meanings are created by the actors but not by the conscious and planned intervention of the sociologist. Nowhere in the book is there even a preliminary discussion of how a scholar with an action orientation might go about changing such variables as individual meanings, the nature of the role-system, the nature of involvement of ideal-typical actors, of the actors' present definition of their situation, etc.

SUMMARY

Our analysis suggests:

(1) Generalizations are made about processes such as the instrumental attitudes of affluent workers. These are, in fact, developed from responses made by *individuals*, which are then aggregated. Once having summed them up they become 'sociological' variables where the individual, as a causal explanation, can be ignored.

The conceptual process by which they go from individual processes to sociological processes is not explicated.

(2) Explaining the basic findings of 'instrumental attitudes' as caused by the employees' reports of their interest in economics is circular.

(3) If individual level variables had been included, the finding of instrumental attitude could be predicted *a priori* and psychological mechanisms posited which would prevent it from being circular. These same variables could be used to explain phenomena such as sociability patterns, to explain which, given the present scheme, the authors must generate additional concepts.

5. IMPLICATIONS

Several points seem worthy of emphasis regarding the implications of this analysis.

(1) It may be inaccurate to state that one can study organizations-as-wholes, if one selects to ignore the admittedly critical parts of organization. Individual's behavior, small group behavior, inter-group behavior, represent important parts that help to create the whole.

Some readers may raise the question of whether we are not misunderstanding the view of the writers by equating organizations as wholes or in the round with whole organization. Perhaps, if one wished to point to the statements that each writer has made to the effect that his approach was only one of many. However, not so, when one reads the discussions these writers develop about the implications of their history.

Moreover, even if this were not the case, the argument that the ignored parts should not be ignored would still appear to be relevant. Even if the authors agreed that they were studying primarily the formal organization (and its congruent technology), there would still be the problem that the data they have obtained are contaminated by, and the generalizations that they make could be influenced by, the very variables that they ignored.

It would be helpful if the writers defined more explicitly what they meant by organizations-as-wholes. Blau, for example, seems to focus, in his empirical data gathering, on the charts of the organization (as modified by discussions with research people and several key discussants). This places him squarely in the tradition of the theories they have characterized as incomplete. As Benoit-Guilbat (1968, p. 234) states: 'In the tradition of F. W. Taylor and above all Max Weber, they [Blau, Selznick, Merton] have specified the conditions for effectiveness of a rational, bureaucratic organization, perfect adaptation of means to ends, and the use of abstract and universal rules. In short, they provide a timely reminder that an organization must give priority to reaching its goals.' The timely reminder provided by the view of Taylor and Weber is that organizations will create difficulties for themselves in reaching their goals, if they limit themselves to formal organizational principles and theory.

The argument is *not* being made therefore, that research must not be partial and incomplete in its view. No one – or any reasonable team – can study a complete organization. The position taken is that if we select a certain aspect to study, such as formal organizations (1) we explain why we are doing so, given the existing literature about that aspect, and (2) include in our theoretical focus (not necessarily in any given empirical study) the variables that are relevant, regardless of their academic discipline.

(2) Researchers would be helped to be reminded of the relevant variables if, in the early stages of their studies (at least), they focussed heavily on directly observable *behavior*. It is interesting to note that those sociologists who focus on behavior are less prone to be interested in dividing their research interests by discipline (e.g. Whyte, Lupton, Woodward, Argyris and Pugh *et al.*, the latter in their theoretical work).

The focus on behavior would make it less easy for the present authors to divide the world up into sociology and psychology and to ignore the individual level of analysis. As we have seen, doing so leads to certain unintended dysfunctionalities in research. For example, circular generalizations are developed, explanations for 'sociologically oriented' correlations are made that include psychological variables that have been excluded. Also, recent research suggests that people may be 'programmed' through early childhood acculturation to hold certain values about effective human relationships. These values result in the development of pyramidal structures and interpersonal relationships with the same properties (Argyris 1968). One of the most frequently documented phenomenon in *T* groups is the reaction of people to the unstructuredness of a *T* group. For the first decade or so (when the educational value of the unstructuredness was not generally known) people overwhelmingly and forcefully reacted to the lack of structure in a *T* group by creating miniature pyramidal organizations to manage the *T* group. Thus in a system that has all the properties of Perrow's number two system (organic) and thus where flexible polycentralized relationships would be expected, the people attempted to create systems that were closer to the routine, formalized, centralized type four.

Our data and analysis confirm Homans' view of the importance of the psychological level of analysis (Homans 1964, 1967). However, I am not ready to grant the psychological explanation the primacy that he is apparently willing to give it. I would prefer a view of reality where the sociological and psychological level variables interact and reinforce each other. The pure psychological approach tends to lead to views of man that ignore the constraints culture and social structures make and thus results in ignoring the deep psychological issues involved in making a continual choice to give up aspects of one's individuality and autonomy in order to maintain one's uniqueness and freedom.

(3) The predominant mode of analysis is the static correlational mode. This can bring insights but can be stultifying if the processes in organization that mediate between the predictor and criterion variables are ignored. To the extent that leadership styles, executive interpersonal relationships, group dynamics and intergroup dynamics influence the variable under consideration they have been placed in a black box status. I would like to quote Blau on this issue, 'It is not enough to indicate, as Weber did, that bureaucratization facilitates substitution of personnel or that impersonal performance standards and impartial treatment of clients tend to occur together in bureaucracies. It is also important to know the processes that account for the association between these factors' (Blau 1968, p. 303). If the sociologists would turn to the field of child development, personality and individual differences (the foundation for testing and selection), they can find ample historical evidence that correlational studies have long-range pay-off toward the development of logically consistent empirically tested theories relevant to the non-contrived ongoing world.

(4) Another possible dysfunctionality is that the nature of man implicit in the research is one of a mechanistic closed-system. Man is not conceptualized as proactive but as passive with little influence on the organization. The individual is treated as a non-human item almost to the point of being conceived of as a black box. Kluckman suggests that this may be a characteristic of much sociological research (1959, p. 253). However, some of the more recent experiments in new kinds of organizational structures have been developed because managers and some behavioral scientists have realized the potentiality of man and the value of redesigning systems to respect and draw upon these potentialities (e.g. matrix organizations, System IV and theory *Y*).

Blau, Thompson, Perrow and Goldthorpe *et al.* imply a concept of man which is very close to the one autocratic conservative management have always maintained; namely that people prefer to be market-oriented and economically oriented. Thus Goldthorpe *et al.* suggest that man is predominantly instrumental in orientation but do not explore the potency of the intrinsic orientation (for the individual) given the fact that it surfaced so strongly with workers who were, by their own analysis, instrumentally oriented. Blau suggests one way to make life more meaningful for an employee is to develop such clear-cut and complete rules that he doesn't have to experience uncertainty nor will the organization run the risk of his gumming up the works.

(5) The criticism that sociologists have made about the early work of the 'human relations' school may now apply to them. Etzioni, for example, suggests that the dangers of this research are that it could adopt management's attitudes and strive to placate the workers and make them passive. Also there was the danger of conflict being suppressed and the system designed and managed primarily in the interests of management (1964, pp. 42–3). These seem to be real dangers with the research discussed above. One could derive from the Goldthorpe *et al.*, Blau, and Thompson works, ways for the organization to 'homogenize' people but pay them well in line with their instrumental attitudes and economic motives.

Another way in which these writers have become, unintentionally, in favor of management is that they have tended to develop generalizations about appropriate fit between organization and the environment that correlates with existing criteria of success. Thus, organic systems are 'best' for turbulent environment, complex technologies etc. Mechanistic systems are 'best' for simple routine technologies and benign environment. How do we know? Because we correlate it with existing production or financial results. Now one could seriously question the rigorousness of the production and financial data used as criterion variables in many of these studies. But, even if this were not so, one certainly could question whether there were not many causal processes ruled out in relating these two variables together (Likert 1967). As we have pointed out, management is increasingly wishing to take organizations with simple and routine technologies and create turbulence at least within the system, in order to reduce some of its dry rot and increase its flexibility. They are aware that 'appropriate' balances between system and environment could lead to stagnation. Also behavioral scientists have shown that it takes a great deal of time to change a system from a mechanistic to a more organic one. Thus, the writers above are in the pro-management camp of traditional managers and not with those who are developing matrix organizations or management information technology which inevitably leads to more organic relationships.

To state this another way, modern line executives tackle these questions by conceptualizing the problem differently for all these scholars. They say (a) there are no *a priori* independent or dependent variables but only mutually dependent variables, and (b) the task of management is to manipulate these variables in order to prevent the organization from being surprised by the environmental change; keep the organization continuously on the alert to change, to manage the transition so that survival is possible. For example, differentiation between units in an organization does not simply vary according to dimensions Lawrence and Lorsch have presently identified (e.g. task complexity and uncertainty in the environment). It may also vary with how management feels about the effectiveness of its own management processes and the effectiveness of the organization.

This interpretation provides a partial explanation for the Allen findings that, contrary to the Lawrence and Lorsch prediction, the degree of differentiation may vary according to the felt need for joint decision making (Allen 1970, p. 27). When the felt need is low the degree of differentiation does not appear to be a potent variable. When the felt need for joint decision is high, then the degree of differentiation is a potent variable. The point is that the conditions vary according to management's view of what is needed if they are going to be leading or managing the system effectively.

Perrow (1970, p. 16) suggests that the formal organizational school is 'fighting a rearguard action in the groves of academe (and perhaps) in the stony fields of actual organizations'. I would agree and wonder if the writers discussed to date are aware to what extent they may be in the rearguard?

SOME EXAMPLES OF RESEARCH PARTIALLY ELUDING THESE PROBLEMS

Below we discuss several sociologists (or sociologists-psychologists) who are conducting research on similar problems and who, with differing degrees of success, are not being plagued by these problems.

An example of research workers who have sociological perspective and have been at least able to enlarge their perspective to include data from other levels is Hage and Aiken (1969, 1970). In the first study they developed measures that included individuals' perceptions of technology and related them to social structure. With the exception of several errors (e.g. they state that routine work leads to formalization when the data is correlational) they seem to have tested some of Perrow's hypotheses effectively. They found some held up and some did not.

In their book, they attempted to separate the psychological and sociological levels. They maintained that the psychological approach viewed organizations as an aggregate of individuals, each with his own abilities, interests, behaviors and motives. Sociological approach viewed organizations as a collective of jobs, each with its own skills, powers, rules and rewards. I confess difficulty with this classification for two reasons. First there are many key psychologists in organizational behavior who are interested in what Hage and Aiken describe as the sociological approach (e.g. Kahn, Likert, Tannenbaum and Schein). Secondly, the measures of routineness that Hage and Aiken used in the study above were precisely measures obtained by conceiving of people as an aggregate with individual responses and interests. Are they implying there is something sociological about an aggregate of individual perceptions? If so, what is it? Later in the same book, the authors state that they have much in common with the 'human relations' approach that emphasizes power equalization. However, their preference 'is to discuss those phenomena in the context of organizational properties' (Hage and Aiken 1970). What organizational properties do they include that are not included by the people who have published research on power equalization?

Finally they say that the power equalization approach emphasizes how to create and bring about change. They say this is a legitimate area of interest but it is beyond the scope of their book. This is a crucial point about the thrust of sociological thinking. In a book about social change in complex organizations, the *creation* of change is beyond its scope! To be sure all scholars have the right to define limits for their work. But these limits may help us to diagnose the state of the field. For example, it is not a random occurrence that all the researchers quoted so far have invoked these limits.

There are three dangers involved in these limits which may be worth consideration. First, as we shall see, it denies the possibility of testing theories under the most demanding conditions, namely to use them to create or change the phenomena or variables under study. Secondly, there is the danger and the one that the authors fall into, of defining some how-to-do-it information (for example, in their chapter on stages and strategies for change) even though they say it is beyond the scope of their book. Finally if sociologists working at the heart of our society (for organizations are the key building blocks) do not become interested in creating and researching change, they will leave our society to the militants and activists, who sometimes give me the impression that one of the first steps they would take if they had power would be to stop scholarly research of the kind Hage and Aiken produce.

In discussing the work of Perrow, I suggested that, given his partial approach to organization, it was possible that his measures for the impact of technology could be contaminated by the impact of leadership styles, administrative controls etc. Lacking examples of items used it was difficult to illustrate this point. However, Hage and Aiken provide one example of a set of items to measure routineness of work which illustrates my point. They measured individuals' perception of the routineness of work by asking them to respond to items (Hage and Aiken 1969, p. 368).

(1) People here do the same job in the same way every day.
(2) One thing people like around here is the variety of work (reversed).
(3) Most jobs have something new happening every day (reversed).
(4) There is something different to do every day (reversed).

The writers expected that the respondents would answer these questions in terms of their job, separating out the great influence that a supervisor's behavior or production bogeys or quality control rule can have on the degree of sameness, variety, something new, etc. happening, while working on the job. Some respondents probably were able to do so. However, cases have been reported where this has not been the case (Argyris 1960, Goldthorpe *et al.* 1969). Do not the authors need to control for this possibility? In the case of the Hage and Aiken study, these types of problems are compounded by the fact that the jobs studied were highly non-routine, and as Perrow points out, were more susceptible to influences by variables other than technology.

In a quotation (p. 369) we note one staff member saying that 'no two days are alike because we deal with highly unpredictable children. We individualize very highly here, we would turn the place upside down for one child . . .' Is it not possible that in some other centers supervisors would exist who would not permit the individualized attention? We may recall (in the Perrow section) that the studies of the treatment versus custodial centers showed different leadership and administrative controls and these, in turn, influenced the routineness of the work of the staff and the life of the inmates. Hage and Aiken appear to examine dimensions related to these questions when they say that they studied dimensions such as job codification, rule observation, but no data are presented that the subjects agree with their assertion that 'clearly routineness is different from the content of each of these' (p. 368). The authors refer the readers to two articles that contain discussions of their measures. One, their own, contains no examples of items used or factor analysis of such items (Aiken and Hage 1968). The other article, a very interesting one, presents one item from each scale (Hall 1963). The one related to authority states, 'A person can make his own decision without checking with anyone else' (p. 35). Assuming the respondent did not know that the item was designed to measure perceptions about authority, could not the respondent, or his supervisor, be influenced by the nature of the technology? It is not uncommon for supervisors in the same department to have different leadership styles (production centered versus people centred, concern for structure versus people). Thus the amount of checking a worker is required to do may not be due to the authority a supervisor has but to his style. Thus the problem where routineness measures may be contaminated by other variables is now illustrated with how organizational authority can be contaminated by leadership styles.

Another group that seems to the writer to desire to develop a more integrated approach is represented by Pugh and Hickson *et al.*

They began their early work with a careful analysis of the relevant literature not being confined to any one academic discipline (Pugh *et al.* 1963). This literature search played a major role in developing their measures. It also led to interesting theoretical articles that attempted to develop theoretical frameworks that integrated several disciplines (Pugh 1966). Their empirical research seems to have less constraints placed on it by an urge to be sociological or psychological or any other discipline. They also seem to study organizations of a wider range than have Blau, Thompson, Hage and Aiken, and (less so) of Perrow (who has continued to broaden his empirical studies). Also their analysis is more differentiated. For example, in a recent study they show that the operations technology affects those structural variables immediately impinged on by the workflow. Thus the smaller the organization the more completely its structure is pervaded by the immediate effects of technology (Hickson, Pugh and Pheipey 1969).

One question that may be raised about this group is related to a criticism Pugh made recently of industrial psychologists. He criticized them for having predictor and criterion variables, conducting all sorts of correlational studies, yet keeping the organizational processes that 'connect' the two in a black box status (Pugh 1966). The same may be said for Pugh's work. His latest thrust of correlating some of his basic dimensions to productivity data continues the early correlational studies approach that keeps the processes in a black box status. I should like to repeat the plea that these authors page through the literally thousands of correlational studies of child development, personality testing and selection and see the paucity of pay-off for the development of explanatory and empirically validated theory. A second plea would be for Pugh and his group to divert more attention to a periodic re-examination of their total theoretical framework as Pugh has done so well for the work of others.

During a recent discussion Pugh told the writer, 'What I want to do is measure. I am willing to borrow others' theories (if it is helpful in order to develop sound empirical generalizations).' In a recent review of research at the core of industrial psychology, it was shown that because of their strong interest in measurement they have tended to place organizational processes in a black box status and be atheoretical in their approach (Argyris 1971). It is always a difficult question to ask when a field becomes too focussed on measurement, but perhaps these two consequences of 'black box' and atheoreticalness are useful operational criteria.

Etzioni has produced several important books that stress the importance of systematic action-oriented research and conceptual schemes crossing traditional academic boundaries (1961, 1969). An example of the latter is the much-quoted typology for classifying organizations. His basic variables are the type of power or authority which the organization uses and the type of involvement which the organizational member has with the organization. Organizations that are predominantly coercive tend to promote an alienative involvement, those that are predominantly utilitarian tend to promote a calculative involvement, and those that are predominantly normative tend to produce a moral involvement. Etzioni maintains that the type of personal involvement depends to a large extent on the kind of power or authority used by the organization.

The typology above represents 'pure' types of systems which Etzioni is careful to point out do not actually exist. Most organizations, at any given time, are probably complex mixtures of these types and may vary in their use of power over time, depending upon pressures for survival, etc.

Although the scheme presented by Etzioni focusses on the sociological and psychological levels, there is a minimum of discussion regarding the latter level. For example, as in the case of Perrow's work on reformatories, Etzioni does not make explicit his assumptions about the nature of human beings when he predicts that coercive power develops alienative involvement. Why should utilitarian organization tend to promote calculative orientations among individuals? What are the processes by which these different influences occur?

Another gap in the use of this interesting typology is the strategy for change one could derive from this typology. For example, one might identify the strategies by which a power orientation can be changed in order to produce a different type of involvement. Studies where the scholars help to plan and execute systemic changes can be, as pointed out repeatedly, important strategies for testing aspects of the typology; for example, the congruence assumptions (between power use and individual involvement) could be tested more rigorously and the processes of influence be made more explicit and probably deepened if Etzioni could conduct studies to show how an organization could be helped to alter the way it uses its power (e.g.

from coercive to utilitarian). One could then observe to see if the involvement is altered from alienative to calculative. It could be, for example, that a calculative orientation would not become a reality where the alienative orientation has been held so long that a large and long-range individual change program might be needed to help individuals surface the issues and make more conscious decisions about their future.

Woodward and her group seem, to the writer, to have been least influenced by the problems discussed above. In the early writing Woodward fell into the trap of inferring behavior from variables that said nothing about the behavior being predicted. For example, she stated, 'management by committee was more common in process industry than in less complex systems'. From this she concluded 'that in many process industries the chief executive functioned more as a chairman of a decision-making body than as an authoritarian decision maker' (Woodward 1965, p. 53). The writer has presented analyses of tape recordings of top management groups which included some from process industries where management by committee was indeed the rule. Yet he found all the chief executive officers functioning as authoritarian decision makers and what's more, the subordinate officers encouraging this (Argyris 1968).

Also, as in the case of Thompson, the Woodward group's early analyses focussed on 'constrained behavior' more than constraint-exceeding or facility-enhancing behavior (Reeves, Turner, Barry and Woodward 1970, p. 12). However, they are aware of this limitation and propose a theoretical framework to help them develop research in this area. I predict that these studies will bring them more in contact with psychological level variables, a level which some members are interested in and use with insight (e.g. Rackman and Woodward 1970, pp. 141–5).

Thus in the second book Professor Woodward and other members of the group continue the qualities of careful analyses, willingness to respect and portray the complexity of the real world, clinical insights and judicious use of quantitative analysis. They seem to be more centered on their problem and on actual behavior than on maintaining a particular academic discipline.

The first step in the new book was to question the older studies as a jumping-off point for new research. Brewer, in an appendix of the first book, developed a scale of increasing rates of production.

He concluded that some firms in Woodward's batch category were 'closer to either continuous flow or unit production firms than they were to each other' (Woodward 1970). Next they asked if variation of product range and the number of production stages may not be more effective differentiating categories (Rackman and Woodward 1970). More research was conducted to illuminate these questions. Finally they began to wonder if variety (i.e. the degree of uncertainty and unpredictability) was not the key variable as the causal link between technology and organizational behavior. They asked if one function of the social system may not be to help make the technical system more effective by dealing with what it cannot deal with, for example, uncertainty and unpredictability.

Woodward and her colleagues suggest that 'the function of the social system is to do what the technical system cannot or has not been designed to do'. I should like to ask designed for whom? Individuals? Groups? Or for what purpose? The control of behavior? I believe the Woodward group would say for people, groups and for the control of behavior. Then perhaps the question to be asked is what is the optimum balance of contributions between the technical and social systems so that the organizations are most effective? Asking the question in this manner permits the additional possibility that the technical systems, at times, may have to be designed to do what the social system cannot do. If one accepts this view, then it also becomes possible to say that another function of the social system is to handle over-certainty and over-routineness (if the technology cannot cope with it). With this level of conceptualization one can predict the possibility that students and assembly line workers have a similar world by measuring the relative over-certainty and over-routineness (as perceived by individuals) in the assembly line and in the classroom.

This approach makes variety a subjective variable. The Woodward group prefer to keep variety an objective variable and then study the subjective correlated to it. As in the case of the scholars discussed above, if they take this route then they will have to specify the mechanisms by which a given objective measure of variety is 'experienced' or 'perceived' by discussion of possible mechanisms in the work of Barker and Wright in psychological ecology. There they attempt to explicate how 'behavioral settings' can get into the life space of individuals (Barker and Wright 1955).

6. APPLICABLE AND APPLIED BEHAVIORAL SCIENCE

The second objective of this study is to attempt to shed some light on how behavioral science research can be made more applicable and applied. According to the dictionary, applicable means to be relevant, pertinent, and germane. Knowledge that is relevant has a traceable connection with the phenomena under consideration. Knowledge that is germane is so closely related to the subject that its fitness is beyond question. Knowledge that is pertinent is so decisively relevant and germane that it touches or identifies the real point at issue or contributes materially to the understanding of the subject under inquiry.

These characteristics suggest that applicable knowledge may be used to understand and comprehend the phenomena under inquiry. To understand and comprehend means to have a clear idea or conception of the knowledge necessary to judge what is relevant, pertinent, and germane about the phenomena under inquiry.

The word applied means to use, to employ, to utilize the knowledge. To use, to employ, means to serve or be able to serve an end or purpose. In order for knowledge to serve some ends or purposes it, at least, must be applicable to those purposes. Thus applied knowledge is knowledge that is applicable and is actually being used.

As the history of behavioral science knowledge can show, the attribute of applicability can be distinguished from what is applied. For example, a recent review of industrial psychology (Argyris 1971a) suggests that there is much in that field that is being applied which may not be applicable to the entire scope of the real or non-contrived world to which the field purports to be germane. The applicability of many of the concepts may be primarily related to the equilibrium or *status quo* aspects of reality rather than to the dynamics or change of reality. In this book, it has been suggested that much of the sociological theory discussed (unintentionally) may be focussing on helping and maintaining the *status quo* as conceived by scientific management. Moreover, because of the one-sidedness and incompleteness of both industrial psychology and sociology, the knowledge may actually be harmful to organizations and human beings. In the case of the latter, the industrial psychologists and sociologists may have created a body of knowledge that ignores or de-emphasizes human potentialities for growth, commitment and change. In the case of the former, the same knowledge may ignore or de-emphasize the possibilities of creating new kinds of organizational forms.

On the other hand, a field of consulting or intervention has been slowly evolving that is applicable. However, the values, goals, and behavior implicit in this theory deviate so strongly from present practice that it is considered by many practitioners and clients as unreal, idealistic, and therefore difficult to apply (Argyris 1970a). This is not an unusual state of affairs in the helping professions especially during the early stages when practice rarely is guided by existing knowledge derived from research. In the field of medicine, for example, as research-based knowledge began to be produced, medical practices became possible that were beyond the competence of many practitioners and, in some cases, not trusted by many patients. The practitioners and patients continued to apply knowledge that was no longer applicable.

The fundamental assumption in this position is a rather simple one. The applicability and utility of knowledge are criteria that should be integrated and given equal potency in the development of behavioral science theories and the execution of such empirical research. If these criteria are fully integrated then an instance of knowledge being applied becomes also a test of its applicability. Such validated application becomes an act of 'basic' research in the sense that it tests the validity of a hypothesis derived from a theory. It may also set the stage for the modification or the development of new theoretical frameworks and empirical research. Finally, whenever knowledge is both valid and applicable it enlarges the potential help that it can give mankind.

Although the assumption that we should focus on developing knowledge which is both applicable and applied to the non-contrived, real world is simple, its execution is extremely complex. The scholar is traditionally rewarded for staying within his discipline even if, as is the case of Blau and Perrow, he can state clearly and explicitly the inherent limitations of his admittedly restricted focus. Moreover, as has been recently suggested, we lack the empirical methodology that combines rigor with vigor (Kelman

1968). Also given the conditions above, it may not be too surprising to hypothesize that the academic behavioral sciences may attract people whose personalities, values, and interpersonal skills would not lead them toward conducting research that is both applicable and applied. Finally, there is the reason that is basically a self-fulfilling prophecy; a field that does not focus on developing knowledge that may be applicable and applied does not tend to develop the knowledge and technology required to achieve this objective.

KNOWLEDGE REQUIRED TO MAKE BEHAVIORAL SCIENCE KNOWLEDGE MORE APPLICABLE AND APPLIED

In striving to understand the requirements involved in making behavioral science knowledge more applicable and applied several key issues arise. The first is how can one produce valid information from studies that have relevance to the non-contrived world? This question is especially pertinent for field studies. How is it possible to test knowledge in field settings sufficiently rigorously for the results to be used with an adequate degree of confidence? This is not a new question. The rigorousness of research activity has concerned behavioral scientists for years and many scholarly works exist that discuss the problems. Our focus will be on the connections between rigorous testing and creating social change.

The second question is related to the form in which knowledge is made available. Are there forms in which knowledge is presented which may increase the probability of its being used more effectively? After all, we have learned that mathematics and languages can be taught more effectively if organized in certain ways. Why should this not be true for behavioral science generalizations? The issue, as we shall see, is extremely complex if 'packaging' is understood to mean going beyond the veneer and the outer cover. We are interested in the basic form and content that makes knowledge applicable. This is a very difficult subject and can only be touched upon in this discussion. It requires systematic inquiry into how man learns, processes information, maintains or strives to increase his sense of competence, and his feelings of self-confidence.

Once knowledge is generated and packaged, the third question that arises is how it should be conveyed to the potential user and how he should use it. These issues focus on the processes of intervention and consulting. The effective use of valid knowledge that is correctly packaged can be wrecked by incorrect intervention methods. Again we are faced with an important area that has hardly been explored. Indeed, if academics were to be honest, they would have to admit that most have viewed consulting as second-rate activities to be, at best, handled cavalierly and, at worse, to be ignored. Yet, if we are to be concerned about applicability, we will have to concern ourselves with the processes of intervention and consulting just as the medical profession realized many decades ago.

Finally, there is the thorny question implicit in the criticism made about industrial psychology and sociology. If they both serve the *status quo*, i.e. the people in power in the non-contrived ongoing world, and if knowledge should serve all groups, and if groups have different views of reality, how does the behavioral scientist go about defining the reality that should concern him?

I do not presume to discuss these important issues with the degree of completeness that they deserve. To do so requires competence in areas that I do not have. Moreover, research in these areas is practically non-existent. The objective of this last section will therefore be to outline these issues and suggest how they may be connected with the sociological research discussed in the first part.

TESTING HYPOTHESES IN FIELD SETTINGS AND CREATING CHANGE

There are several ways to test any theory in a field setting. The first is to derive predictions from the theory about what one should find under given conditions, then go into the non-contrived world, locate such conditions and note if the predicted consequences actually occurred.

A second method is to make *a priori* predictions of what one would find under a differential set of conditions. This includes comparative studies, namely, the study of systems under different conditions. It also includes the study of change over time that is created by forces not under the direct or indirect influence of the researcher.

The third, and most rigorous test of a theory, is to be able to create the conditions hypothesized; to create the variables, and to predict *a priori* what should happen. The third mode is the most rigorous because it involves the researcher in generating, managing, and controlling the variables under consideration. The researcher is taking on a relationship with the non-contrived world that is similar to the one the experimental behavioral scientist takes with the experiments he plans and executes. The most rigorous form is when changes are created under different conditions, one of which being the control condition. In actual practice control organizations are extremely difficult to create in a field setting. The next best solution may be to develop a time-series design where the organization is studied carefully before, during, and after the change. However, this too is fraught with difficulties since there are so many possible variables and interrelationships that may act to inhibit or facilitate the intended manipulation of specific variables.

The complexity and uncertainty however need not necessarily sentence us to non-action. As will be suggested later on, complexity and uncertainty are phenomena that human beings face continually. One way to begin to manage these phenomena is to create heuristics or cognitive maps which, after long experimentation, become theoretical frameworks guiding the individual in his actions. The researcher can also develop theoretical frameworks. Indeed, he may have much more knowledge about the technology of building theoretical frameworks. The objective of these frameworks would be to make it possible for the researcher to identify the critical variables that may be required if the change is to occur and those that will require continuous monitoring if the change is to be thoroughly understood. The point being made so far is that studies of change *created* and *managed* by the researcher represent one of the most rigorous tests for a theory and provide guideposts of what needs to be included in the theory if it is to be relatively complete and applicable.

Let us hypothesize that Blau was to go into a field situation where he was permitted to *create* changes that would lead to further testing of his theory. How may such studies be designed?

One possible study would be to test the empirical relationships which, Blau claims, exist between size and differentiation. In this study, he would have to create the different size units and the differentiation within each unit. How would he go about differentiating the units? His formal theory does not include any generalizations about the basis of differentiation. Nevertheless Blau is aware that formal organizations have explicit procedures for systematically subdividing the work. He states, 'different tasks are assigned to different positions; specialized functions are allocated to various divisions and sections' (Blau 1970, p. 216). Where do these procedures come from? They are derived directly from the principles of job specialization, unity of command and chain of command. In order to design the study Blau would have to identify these traditional management principles and make explicit that he is differentiating the organization according to their requirements. Any generalizations that would come out of this research would naturally be linked to the conditions under which differentiation occurred, namely the traditional management principles. Thus Blau would find himself making explicit the conditions under which his generalizations held, namely the traditional management principles and not size.

Such research would fulfill one of the criteria discussed above, namely, to create, manage, and predict change under a given set of conditions. A more difficult criterion to fulfill, but one that would lead to a more rigorous test of the theory, would be to vary the conditions under which differentiations occur. If Blau were to attempt this he would immediately face the challenge of designing organizations that did *not* depend upon the existing formal procedures, because to limit himself to the existing formal procedures would be to limit the variance possible in the conditions. This would mean that a new system of procedures for the design of organizations would have to be created. What would these procedures look like? What assumptions would they be based upon that are different from those upon which the present formal procedures are based?

The exploration of these questions naturally surfaces the assumption implicit in the present procedures for designing organizations. One sub-set of assumptions, illustrated in the work of Blau, Thompson, Perrow, Goldthorpe and Lockwood *et al.*, is that psychological man may be conceptualized as a black box. Another set of assumptions, also illustrated in the work of Blau, Thompson, and Cyert and March, is that the organization's design and its management activities result primarily from complex factors such as 'price structure', 'engineering economics', or 'satisficing'.

A third sub-set of assumptions is related to the environment. Initially, scholars had considered the environment as non-relevant or benign. Scholars such as Burns, Lawrence and Lorsch conducted research from which they concluded that the environment, far from being benign, was critical in determining the design of the internal structure. Unfortunately, instead of these scholars focussing on how individuals, groups and intergroups act to perceive and manage, and change, the environment and vice versa, the 'new' push was to start the old polarizing process over again. As Lawrence has stated it, 'Tell me what is your environment and I will tell you what your organization ought to be' (personal communication).

Incidentally these three assumptions suggest three examples of how behavioral science knowledge may implicitly embrace a normative position which is not only questioned by existing empirical research, but may be repugnant to the very scholars who have created them. As pointed out in Part I, these assumptions view man as being passive and reactive, or as being primarily interested in the 'conditions of rationality', or 'satisficing', so that he may prefer dull work and little use of his important abilities, as well as to be controlled by supervisors and budgets *if* he can be paid adequately for it. The 'market orientation' generated by human beings to adapt to organizations is now embedded in these theories and, if they are used by someone as a basis for action, will be reinforced.

Do not behavioral scientists have some responsibility to make explicit the fact that their theories may include a view of the nature of man that has neither received empirical confirmation nor has ever been declared immutable and unchangeable? Does not the theorist have some responsibility to state explicitly why he accepts certain, and excludes other, views of the nature of man?

Some readers may react that discipline-oriented scholars have usually been explicit about their assumptions. Most have rarely claimed that their knowledge is applicable and applied. Most have carefully delimited the range of applicability of their knowledge. To this the writer would reply, by using the works of Blau, Thompson and Perrow, that scholars do make these disclaimers at the beginning and end of their work. However, in the middle they do tend to fall into generalizations about practice. Moreover, as we shall see below, some go on to develop theories of change and try them out in ways that raise issues about the credibility of their disclaimers.

Recently, some researchers have begun to ask what organizations would look like if they were designed and managed according to strategies that considered their needs as relevant as economic, engineering and internal political variables. For example, some researchers have attempted to develop a new set of formal organizational design procedures by making a different set of assumptions about the nature of man and his motivation. They inferred these assumptions from existing descriptive research generated in the field of personality and development in our culture. This had led to organizational design procedures quite different from those that Blau, Thompson and Perrow utilize. For example, different tasks are assigned to the same (not different) position, specialized functions are redesigned into more molar units and grouped into one unit (not different units), the administrative components are decreased (not enlarged) (Argyris 1964, Ford 1969, McGregor 1960, Gooding 1970).

Predictably these new assumptions were not easily accepted by employers, by employees or, as we shall see, by many scholars. The workers understandably wondered if they could trust management and questioned the wisdom of becoming more involved in work, especially if they had opted for the market-orientation or instrumental view of life. The employers feared that more organic structures required much more trust and openness among management personnel than presently existed. Many in both groups questioned seriously, in response to questions and questionnaires, whether organizational design should include more humanistic assumptions. Such data led scholars, who conceived of their research objectives as describing reality, to conclude that employers and employees questioned the advisability of designing organizations and managing them in a manner that gave added potency to personality type variables. What these scholars tended to ignore was the point made repeatedly in this analysis that descriptive studies tend to accept the normative views implicit in the *status quo*.

In spite of the resistance by all three groups the research on new designs has continued, partly because the researchers have a scientific interest to learn more by creating new organizational forms, partly because they believed they had data to show that the present forms were creating worse dysfunctional conditions for both employee and employer, and partly because of personal values that organizational designs should explore, taking more account of human beings when they were designing new systems and when executives were managing such systems.

However, for the purposes of this discussion one could still argue for the development of such models and the conduct of such research without the interest in wanting organizations to be more concerned about human beings. Remaining strictly at the level of motivation for scientific inquiry and progress, the argument can be made that these new organizational forms provide a new set of conditions to test existing theories. Thus the argument is *not* being made that a more 'personality-based' organization is necessarily more effective. It remains for empirical research to confirm or disconfirm this hypothesis. The suggestion is being made that such research be conducted because it would help, for example, Blau (1) to specify all the possible conditions under which his theory would not hold (2) to concern himself with developing a theory that eventually could integrate these findings, and (3) would help to reduce the inconsistencies of his present theory.

A similar argument can be made about Perrow's work. He states that most manufacturing firms fit into the 'quite routine' cell because, 'It is in their interest to fall into this category because it means greater control over processes and much more certainty of outlook' (Perrow 1970, pp. 81–2). If Perrow were interested in testing this proposition (in the field) he might vary the degree of the variables in his quite routine cell and see what happens to control over processes and certainty of outlook. He might find that the relationship is not linear. For example, the research cited above has shown that Perrow's generalization is probably valid *if* man acts in a market-oriented economic-man fashion. The same research suggests that many people resent and resist such attitudes, which leads to behavior on their part which reduces management's control and certainty. The research also suggests that many people *accept* the economic-man outlook and still behave in ways that reduce management's control and certainty (e.g. apathy, indifference, high rejects, wild-cat strikes, rate-setting etc.).

DOES THE FORM IN WHICH KNOWLEDGE IS MADE AVAILABLE INFLUENCE THE PROBABILITIES THAT IT WILL BE USED EFFECTIVELY?

The second issue related to making behavioral science knowledge more applicable and applied is related to the form in which it is organized. This issue has, to the writer's knowledge, received little attention. One possible explanation is that behavioral scientists have assumed that any valid knowledge is potentially applicable and therefore the task of researchers is to concern themselves with validity and preciseness. But do these views represent the problem adequately?

The usability of knowledge is partially a function of its semantic clarity. Although this can be a difficult barrier because all groups (including laymen) have their jargon, let us assume, for the sake of argument, that the problem is soluble if the parties find it worth while to learn each other's language or to reduce their respective quotient of jargon. Beyond this requirement three others must be fulfilled if the behavioral science knowledge is to be used effectively.

A. *The user as a finite information-processing system*

Man cannot use knowledge unless he is able to perceive and understand it. This involves his capacities to think and process information. Bruner's (1971) and Simon's (1969) research suggests that man's capacity to process information is influenced by the following:

(1) The human information-processing system is finite, indeed quite simple and not complex. Complexity exists in the environment.

(2) The system is basically serial in its operation. It processes only a few symbols at a time.

(3) The symbols being processed must be held in special, limited memory structures whose content can be changed rapidly (Simon 1969, pp. 52–3).

(4) Two important capabilities which man has available to him to deal with complexity are the ability to create concepts, hierarchies of concepts, and heuristic strategies that permit him to cut through complexity and to accept a 'satisficing' solution (less than optimal but satisfactory solution).

B. *Man is a system seeking self-acceptance and self-confidence*

During the past two decades a new view of man's basic motivational tendencies has begun to develop. There is an increasing awareness that man seeks to be competent (White 1959), to be growth-oriented (Maslow 1954), to seek novelty (Maddi 1968) and to achieve (McClelland 1953). These conceptions have some basic similarities.

They all see man as seeking to set realistic but risky goals (e.g. exploring novelty), defining the paths to these goals and working to overcome the realistic barriers in order to achieve their goals. The more the individual is able to have such experiences, the higher his level of self-acceptance and self-confidence. The higher the self-acceptance and self-confidence, the lower the probability that the individual can be threatened by valid information or opportunities to define and achieve new goals.

C. *Man is a self-responsible, origin-oriented system*

Closely allied to the need for competence and self-confidence is, according to some scholars, man's basic 'condition' to be responsible for, the origin of, his life activities. This condition is assumed to exist in man whether he is aware of it or not. What prevents the view from becoming a tautology is that predictions can be made about what happens to man who suppresses or denies this basic condition.

Man is 'condemned' not to sin but to be self-responsible (Bugental 1965), to be the origin of his behavior (DeCharms 1968), to be proactive (Allport 1960). Bugental defines responsibility as the experience of being a determinant of what happens (Bugental 1965, p. 23). Guilt is the sense of incompleteness in realizing one's potential (p. 37).

If these are indeed properties of man then the generalizations offered by behavioral scientists should be so stated that they can be used within the constraints created by these properties. The reader may justifiably ask if these properties of man have been proven to be as basic as the writer suggests. Perhaps man's finiteness in information processing may be basic but is there not a serious question with the other two (seeking self-acceptance and striving to be responsible)?

The writer would agree that the research to support all three properties, but especially characteristics B and C, is limited. Moreover characteristics B and C express more about man's potentialities than about the actualities. They represent states of psychological affairs which are correlated with the individual's capacity to learn, to understand complexity and to be less threatened by ambiguity.

One might argue that social science knowledge has a greater probability of being used judiciously by people with relatively high self-acceptance and self-responsibility. Thus it may be strategically sound to design knowledge in such a way that the users of it will be most interested in respecting people's right to choice, and least interested in glossing over complexity.

To summarize: these properties of man represent, at least, potentialities; cultures can be created where they become actuality, and one way to help assure the effective use of social science knowledge is to help design and create a world where more people exhibit more of these characteristics.

One may now ask what are some of the constraints that are placed upon the form of scientific generalizations if they are to be useful to man as he seeks to utilize the above characteristics or to actualize these potentialities while simultaneously to design new organizational forms (thereby modifying the culture). Unfortunately, little research exists on this question. However, some suggestions can be offered.

(1) The number of variables and relationships considered must be adequate to comprehend the complexity of the problem, yet not be beyond the information-processing capacity of the individual under satisficing conditions.

For example, generalizations that variable (a) increases monotonically with increase in variable (b) may be analytically elegant but man will have little or no opportunity to measure any two variables with such precision under real conditions. Moreover, he will probably be faced with complex sets of variables each interacting with each other. Nor are generalizations that arise from multi-variate techniques more helpful. The number of relationships that these generalizations 'require' the individual to juggle simultaneously may be beyond the capacity of the short- or long-term information-processing capacities, again given the real world constraints of time and resources.

To put this another way, scientists spend their time analyzing problems as precisely as possible. In doing so, they ignore real time. For example, the writer has spent ten man-days analyzing a three-hour tape recording. One reason that the writer took ten man-days is due to the fact that his information-processing system is finite and simple and works serially. I had to cope with one or two variables at a time. I ignored real time therefore, and kept working until all the variables were analyzed. This behavior is also congruent with my desire to strive for self-acceptance, feelings of being responsible for new knowledge and success in an analytical mode. But, the human being, including the writer, cannot postpone real time when he is in the action mode. He now needs generalizations in the form that are usable within real time constraints.

Given these constraints, how can knowledge be organized so that it would be useful to man as an activist?

D. *Implications about the form in which knowledge is made available*

(1) Knowledge should be stated in the form of units that are usable by many. Research needs to be conducted concerning the size of unit with which man can deal. It is the writer's experience that much research is stated in units that are much more molecular than the human mind can use effectively. It is as if man is capable of thinking primarily in feet while much research is defined (in order to be rigorous) in inches.

Another possible problem with molecular units is that they may be more volatile than units that are more molar. Litwin and Stringer have found that the more molecular measures were more volatile and that individuals did not tend to carry around in their heads 'specific and molecular expectancies and incentives described in the Atkinson model, but rather react to more general molar impressions of what is likely or possible or valuable in a given situation' (1968, p. 29).

(2) If we were to take seriously the aspirations to develop generalizations such as X varies monotonically with Y, then the number of such generalizations needed to describe accurately the complex multi-variateness of the non-contrived world would probably lead to generalizations which would become as difficult to utilize and manage as (at least) a complex chess game. The reaction of the user will be, according to Simon, to develop heuristics which greatly simplify the generalizations without losing too much of their usability. If so, perhaps we should take more interest in developing the heuristics for the practitioner to assure their proper translation of the rigorous generalization. Developing these heuristics will be no easy task. However, as Simon indicates, it is possible to do so, and in terms of our biases they can become the basis for systematic study. It is beyond the capacity of the writer to state precisely what these heuristics would look like. However, one may conjecture that

they would be statements that take into account man's apparent capacity to overdetermine and to be redundant, to use variables that stand up under conditions of noise or ambiguity. The calculus of heuristics may turn out to be sloppy (compared to precise mathematical formulations). This conjecture may not be too unreal for as Von Neuman has suggested, the capacity to use sloppy categories, and yet make accurate predictions, may be a basic characteristic that distinguishes the human being from other problem-solving unities, be they animal or computer (Von Neumann 1958).

(3) Scientific generalizations may have to be stated in such a way that man is able, given his need to do so, to utilize his capacity to make self-fulfilling prophecies. This means that man may prefer generalizations that specify the variable that is relevant more than the systematic empirical generalizations about relationships among the variables (e.g. *X* varies monotonically with *Y*). He may prefer a theory that specifies the possible relevant variables more than knowledge that generalizes about the potency of the variables. For example, a group of executives preferred the theoretically derived, but empirically untested, generalization (i.e. an hypothesis) such as: 'The higher one goes up the organizational hierarchy, the more potent are the interpersonal relationships, and the less trust will tend to exist among the individuals', to the generalization about the same phenomena that was inferred from empirical research that specified a quantifiable relationship between trust on the one hand, and position in the hierarchy and length of time on the job on the other, as reported in some recent research (Alderfer 1967, Hall and Lawler 1968).

The reason for the preference for the less rigorously tested generalizations was that it apparently provided the executives with the knowledge that they needed to get on with creating their own self-fulfilling prophecies. The more they used generalizations that spelled out rigorously the empirical relationships among the variables, the less they felt that they would attribute success to their efforts; the less therefore, the possibility of psychological success, and thus the less the feelings of competence.

Moreover, given the necessary incompleteness of most generalizations, the executives expect that most behavioral sciences generalizations will tend to be inadequate. Consequently they may prefer decision-making processes where they design the sequence of steps and then elicit corrective feedback and where they define the relationships among the variables so that they can create a self-fulfilling prophecy. Thus a variable may be shown by research to account for 10% of the non-random variance. The executive may wish to structure the world so that he can make the same variable (under the same conditions) account for 80% of the non-random variance.

To say this another way, scientifically rigorous generalizations systematically explaining the world could deprive the users of those very activities (e.g. making self-fulfilling prophecies, setting their own level of aspiration, exploring ambiguity) that could lead to their experiencing psychological success and a sense of competence. This suggestion is not as far out as some readers may believe. Recent research in quantitatively based management information systems (M.I.S.) (which strive to develop rigorous generalizations about the world) may be resisted by managers because they create for them conditions of psychological failure (Argyris 1970b).

Cronbach and Gleser (1965, pp. 145 ff) have differentiated between wide- and narrow-band methods of analysis. The wide-band methods (which tend to be more qualitative and rich) transmit more information but the clarity and dependability of the information may be less than for the narrow-band method. The authors suggest that the wide-band methods may be especially suited for early research and diagnosis where exploration is a primary objective and sequential decisions are possible (i.e. where feedback and correction are possible). The narrow-band method may be more relevant when the objective is to arrive at a terminal decision.

The distinction made by Cronbach and Gleser is relevant to the argument in two ways. First, if the conclusions from the M.I.S. studies are repeated, they suggest that in order to survive practitioners may prefer sequential decision making and resist terminal decisions plus narrow-band methods. They would prefer to keep their options as open and flexible as possible and to receive as much feedback as possible in order to correct for any errors. If so, then one way to make social science results more applicable is to develop models and generalizations that utilize, or are congruent with, wide-band methods and sequential decision making.

In re-examining the question of clinical and statistical prediction, Holt (1970) has argued that if clinical is to be compared with statistical prediction, the best examples of each should be used. This has been done for statistical instruments but not for clinicians.

The same suggestion deserves careful consideration in designing and developing social science knowledge. It may be that the best practitioners will prefer the wide-band to the narrow-band methods while the reverse may be the case for the less effective executives. The latter may prefer terminal decisions made by psychological technology in order to reduce their sense of responsibility and accountability.

ARE THERE METHODS OF INTERVENTION THAT ARE MORE EFFECTIVE THAN OTHERS?

Once knowledge is generated and organized and packaged, one arrives at the point of helping man use it. Until recently, behavioral scientists have not shown much concern about thinking as systematically about their consulting activities as they did about their research activities. This may have been an important error. It may have not only led to poor quality consulting; it may have led to the notion that the process of consulting is probably less important than the quality of the knowledge being transmitted.

We are beginning to see signs that clients are concerned about the values behavioral scientists hold regarding their intervention activities. For example, they are questioning those behavioral scientists who seek to apply their ideas to help the poor, disadvantaged, and those with low power, and do this with intervention processes that are authoritarian and unilateral, thereby keeping the client in a disadvantaged low-power relationship (Zurcher 1970).

Let us assume, in order to illustrate the point, that Blau, Perrow and Thompson did develop a new set of assumptions and, to make their case the strongest possible, these assumptions were not based upon understanding human beings but some new economic-engineering principles. How would they go about unfreezing the old organizations, or creating new one?

In the case of the former, one might say that they might design an organization based upon the new principles and pay people well to induce them to come to work. But how long will that persist? There is increasing evidence, among the young in the management levels and in the more affluent lower level employees, that, after a certain point, the more potent inducements are those relating to a higher quality of life inside the system or more frequent opportunity to leave the system (e.g. absenteeism, shorter hours, sabbaticals etc.).

Returning to the challenge of how would the researchers unfreeze the old organizations to consider the new ones one may ask, would they work at the interpersonal level? Would they involve the employees? Would they utilize group dynamics? If so, what theories of interpersonal and group dynamics would they utilize? How would these theories of change be integrated with their present theories of steady state?

What are the theories of intervention held by the scholars whose work is being considered? This is not an easy question to answer because they have not dealt with it explicitly. However, discussions with Blau, Perrow, Thompson and Goldthorpe suggest that they hold these views about intervention. When I have pressed Blau and Perrow, the model of intervention they presented has been one of feedback of the research results and then an attempt to persuade the hypothetical clients to consider alternative states of affairs. For example, Perrow was willing to recommend a mechanistic system for a routine and simple production system. Goldthorpe would hold lectures for trade unionists telling them where they were misguided in their collective bargaining strategies and urging new strategies based on his findings. When asked for a hypothetical scenario he said that he would begin by telling the union leaders, in effect, that 'you chaps are going about collective bargaining the wrong way. What you are doing is wrong'.[1]

At the conference, during the discussion on this paper, in which sociologists, including Blau, Thompson and Perrow, participated, I asked for suggestions on ways in which change could be brought about by using sociological theory whose change processes did not manipulate people (in the same way, following Weberian theory, people are manipulated within the organization). The response by Meyer (taken from a tape recording of the session) was illustrative of the position taken in this paper. (It is interesting that the three sociologists named above did not disagree with his view.)

'How can we sociologists make changes without manipulating people? And here I am taking a leaf out of Chick Perrow's book. The answer is no you can't. Of course you manipulate people.

[1] Personal communication. It should be pointed out that Goldthorpe was not conducting research with the primary aim of helping the trade unionists or any other group.

But this is one of the lessons which unfortunately social science teaches us.'

The writer responded that 'social science' did not teach this; it was a particular brand of social science. These change strategies assumed the same relationship between researcher and client that traditional or Weberian management assumed about workers. To over-simplify, the change strategies were primarily authoritarian. Again, this is not to say that such strategies are necessarily wrong or proven to be ineffective. It *is* to say that these implications have been kept implicit; that they are not communicated to the reader openly. It is to say that these authoritarian strategies flow from the work of authors who have complained about the early human relations proponents for being manipulators and the protectors of management values. It appears now that they would create the very same state of affairs by their intervention activities.

It is difficult to present detailed empirical evidence for this conclusion because organizational sociologists have not been prolific in their studies of change. The writer was able to find one attempt conducted by Vinter and Janowitz (1961). We have quoted this study above in describing the difference between treatment and custodial systems. Let us now focus on the Vinter–Janowitz strategy for change.

Their strategy for change tends to follow from their theoretical bias. Thus we find that the change process used was to attempt to influence the heads of the institutions. The rationale was that 'the key to organizational effectiveness in our view is executive leadership' (Vinter and Janowitz, p. 42), because it is primarily responsible for the organization's objectives. This theory assumes, as the authors hypothesize, 'A high consistency between executive perspectives and institutional goals' (Vinter and Janowitz, p. 63). This assumption has not only been questioned by previous organizational research but it is questioned by the authors' data. They did not find a one-to-one relationship, for example, between the executives' goal and perspectives and the staff's views of their organization's objectives (Vinter and Janowitz, p. 201).

The change process emphasized the rational and de-emphasized the emotional dimensions. Thus the seminar was primarily one in which the researchers presented their data, clarified questions, posed intellectual challenges, and supplied the executives with cognitive maps that helped them to see their institutions in new ways.

If one conceptualizes the executive seminars as temporary organizations, one may infer that the researchers tended to develop more of a custodial than a treatment type of 'change organization'. The emphasis on rationality, on hypothesizing change based on feeding back information to the people with admittedly different views and perspectives, seems to imply a rather simple and undifferentiated view of the problem of unfreezing the clients. The character of the feedback session as described was one of a class room where the experts were in control defining the agenda, clarifying the research results, and so on. The sessions were designed to help the executives to overcome what the researchers called a 'deficit of information', an assumption consonant to one that was held by the staff in the custodial organization, namely, that delinquents lacked the 'proper' information.

The feedback of information, the researchers state, led many of the executives to realize that they did not know their institutions well. Moreover, the authors continue, the new awarenesses tended to threaten the executives because they began to realize that they were not as competent as they had thought (Vinter and Janowitz, p. 595). As far as one can tell, nothing was done by the researchers to help the executives with their resulting feelings of decreasing worth and administrative incompetence other than to insist that they (the researchers) were not implying that this was bad and at the same time to encourage further analysis, which by the researchers' admission would probably lead to new surprises for the executives and, if they took them seriously, new feelings of incompetence and failure.

Moreover, the writers state that after the feedback of their data, 'one executive crashed his fist on the table and angrily exclaimed that he would not tolerate such sentiments among his staff; another was observed, after the session, bracing his staff driver against the wall and demanding to know how he felt about the institution and its purposes' (Vinter and Janowitz, p. 621). The writers then continue to enlighten the reader as to *how* all this comes about by saying that the executives first became defensive then moved on 'toward sharing experiences about ways for coping with such conditions', and finally 'out of this discussion emerged a more clear and forthright recognition of internal [problems]'.

Initial responses to these findings included attempts to minimize their implications as a 'play on words' (i.e. the meaning of questionnaire wording), or to redefine executive–staff discrepancies as showing how advanced was the leadership of administrators. These attempts were abortive and discussion soon moved toward the sharing of experience about ways for coping with such conditions. Out of this discussion emerged a more clear and forthright recognition of internal problematic conditions and the ineffectiveness of existing executive approaches to these difficulties (Vinter and Janowitz, p. 602).

Another example of the emphasis on the cognitive and the de-emphasis of emotionality occurred when the researchers realized that the executives were beginning to use the data to establish a rank order of institutions which they (the researchers) felt was not supported by the data. 'It appeared self-serving and largely a projection of prevailing beliefs and ideologies', and 'it carried with it evaluate connotations not based upon but relevant to criteria of effectiveness', and, finally, 'premature acceptance of any ranking order would have prejudged and impeded the aims of comparative research'.

How was this defensive reaction on the part of the executives handled? The authors reply, 'The initial ranking system was dissipated only gradually and *primarily through the introduction of more and more findings which challenged its basic premises*' (Vinter and Janowitz, p. 607, italics mine). This concept of the change process would not have tended to exist for the researchers if they had applied their theoretical bases to their own behavior. They imply that the more therapeutic or treatment orientation will probably be more effective in dealing with client change. Would it not have been helpful if they had utilized some of the attributes of the 'treatment' orientation in helping their clients?

Why would researchers develop only essentially authoritarian intervention theories? Before I attempt to answer this question, I should like to surface another question interrelated with this one. Does not the researcher have the right to use any intervention processes as long as they help him to obtain the data that he needs to test his theory?

The key to this question is to specify the conditions which give the researcher the maximum possible assurance that he will get valid data *and* continue to do so. Elsewhere, the writer has suggested that the established modes of rigorous research create a temporary system (between researcher and subject) that is genotypically similar to the system created by the traditional principles of formal organization. It is possible to derive from this viewpoint several major forces acting on subjects (1) consciously or unconsciously to distort or to withhold valid information and (2) to reject increasingly the value of social science research (Argyris 1968).

Now if the change methods used by researchers compound these forces, then existing social science research may be placed into question while such future research may be seriously jeopardized. Thus, the answer appears to be that researchers (as researchers) may not be free to use any intervention methods that they wish. If researchers continue to use the presently mechanistic research methods and if they compound these with authoritarian-oriented change methods they will increase the potential for invalid data and they may hasten the day of the demise of research.

The first answer therefore to the question of why scholars may naturally turn to authoritarian change methods is that education in rigorous research tends to educate scholars to seek to control subjects; to place subjects in situations of psychological failure, dependence and short-time perspective (Argyris 1968).

A second answer is related to the acculturation scholars tend to obtain regarding effective human relationships. Elsewhere, I have suggested that socialization and formal educational processes tend to program human beings with concepts about effective human relationships that inevitably leads them to seek, create, and reward authoritarian relationships – be they leaders, subordinates, or researchers. The pattern of behavior and norms that leads to this indoctrination also tends to lead to a world of low trust, low openness, and low accuracy in perceiving reality especially under conditions when it contains differential power or stress. This, in turn, leads to a world in which individuals tend not to receive valid feedback about their behavior, especially if it is unilaterally controlling others and if the individual has power. Both of these conditions are central to existing methods of rigorous research (Argyris 1968).

HOW IS THE REAL WORLD TO BE DEFINED?

The philosophical and metaphysical problems of defining what is reality are complex and beyond the competence of the writer. For the purposes of this discussion, I should like to suggest the following propositions which, if accepted, will permit the discussion to go beyond the metaphysics.

(1) The real world is infinitely complex.

(2) In order for human beings to make sense of reality, given their finiteness, they will understand it only partially. Each of us will necessarily see only a part of the elephant.

(3) The behavioral science researcher is not responsible for defining for the client what is the correct part of reality that he should strive to understand. The behavioral scientists may be required to be capable of producing valid knowledge about different aspects of reality chosen by different clients.

(4) Once valid information is produced then the behavioral scientist may become an interventionist or consultant. Then his primary tasks become to help the client develop, from the valid information, free and informed choices in order to manage, monitor and be in control over their world (Argyris 1970a).

Recently, some writers have suggested that the behavioral scientist should strive to go beyond developing valid information about the world as it is. Behavioral scientists should consider the responsibility of conducting descriptive, rigorous research about the world as it might be (Argyris 1968, Boulding 1969, Heilbroner 1970, Michael 1968). For example, Heilbroner asks for the 'conversion of economics into an instrument of social science whose purpose and justification was not so much the elucidation of the way society actually behaves, as the formulation of the ways in which it should behave' (1970, pp. 91–2).

In order to understand the forces that are acting on some behavioral scientists to suggest this new additional role for their colleagues, it would be helpful to review briefly some of the differences between the social and physical science universes.

To date we have concluded that scholars may be, like other members of society, educated to create authoritarian unilateral interpersonal relationships (even though they may value more equalitarian modes); that, in the case of scholars, this is carried out by following the requirements of traditional rigorous research procedures. Unlike others, scholars are dedicated to inquiry and the pursuit of valid information. However, the methods they use may ultimately create conditions where the subjects will consciously or unconsciously give invalid information but either be unaware that they are doing so or hide the fact.

This means that the methods of rigorous research can act to tap the defenses of respondents related to being in submissive, dependent situations where they are used for the sake of the creation of knowledge. The result may be that the researcher is faced with a universe whose agents – his subjects – may tend to vacillate in the data they give. This means, unlike the physical science universe, the social science universe may be capricious and play tricks. Moreover the social science universe does not remain open and passive to being studied by rigorous methods. Indeed, the very research methods may cause the universe to respond (through its agents, the subjects) in an unpredictable and fickle manner. Boulding has suggested that as science develops it no longer merely investigates the world, it creates the world which it is investigating (1969, p. 3).

A basic difference between the physical and social universe is that the latter serves a purpose for its members that is both long lasting and immediately changeable. The purpose of the social universe is to provide order and guidelines for some sort of effective life (as defined by the members). One could say that the universe of discourse studied by behavioral scientists represents, at any given time, the 'satisficing' solution for man's way of coping with the problems of maintaining an orderly life.

Unlike the physical science universe, the social science universe may be, and is, modified by participants. Indeed, the way members can devise if they even exist as parts of the universe is to be able to alter it. It is this continual conscious change of reality that provides the bases for man to know that he is 'in control' of his life.

Turning to the researcher, it was our position above that he too illustrated or confirmed his understanding of the universe in proportion to his ability consciously to manage and control the variables within his scientific interest. Thus problem-centered action-oriented research was a necessary activity in developing valid theories about the most basic aspects of human social life. This possibility is not unknown to behavioral scientists. Holmberg and his associates bought an entire village which they then systematically changed to give the population increasing control over their everyday lives and long-range destiny (Holmberg 1955). More recently Etzkowitz has suggested a field of institution formation sociology. He would ask sociologists to involve themselves in social reform and resolving societal crises (Etzkowitz

1970). A major department of psychology has developed a Ph.D program for students interested in creating change (Tornatzky, Fairweather and O'Kelly 1970). Argyris (1970a) and Denzin (1970) warn that this will not be easy and conclude that the best applied work will come when the behavioral scientists have a significant input about what is studied, how it is studied, and what is to be done with the findings. As such change studies increase, the capacity to speak of causal factors and resolution of problems will also increase. Under these conditions, as Reiss suggests, behavioral science can be put into policy (Reiss 1970).

If researchers do not conduct research that creates change (in order to study it) the study of change will be left to those who are willing to be activists whether they have sound knowledge or not. Such people can create more difficulties and greater problems. Ironically, society may be more ready to excuse them than the descriptive oriented behavioral scientist because the activists may be seen, at least, to care for society. The researcher may be ignored or actively condemned however, because his apparent disinterest may be viewed by the citizen as researchers playing their research violins while society was burning.

One reason, therefore, why mankind may be so protective about managing its universe is that the social universe exists because man wills it to be the case. Man is basically responsible for the nature of the social world that he has created and his survival in it. It is this realization of responsibility that may make man protective and conservative toward social research. The conservative attitude may be functional however, because it may help to motivate the researcher to conduct careful research and seek well documented generalizations. The conservative stance may also be harmful because it could lead to restricting or inhibiting progress in research. This possibility may best be overcome by the establishment of effective dialogue and trust between the researcher and the subject. But, as we have indicated previously, one of the forces that inhibits the development of open dialogue and trust is related to the temporary universe or existential situation created by rigorous research methods.

Accepting the idea that action research and basic research may be inseparable does not necessarily require that the researcher play God and tell people what to do. Indeed, as noted above, people may well resist being told what to do by experts, be they behavioral scientists or management scientists or operations researchers. Man may seek information about the costs and benefits of different normative states of affairs. He may prefer, however, to select in which state of affairs he will live. Thus clients may like to have research on the kinds of organizational designs that may enhance different states of integration of human beings and organizations. However, they may prefer to choose which of these affairs should exist for them.

Another important consequence of separating studies of steady-state change may be illustrated in the works of Blau, Perrow, and Thompson. In all three cases we have suggested that they are actually taking a normative position, that they appear unaware of this possibility, namely that their position is in favor of the present orthodoxy. Their theorizing depends upon, and tends to be limited to, the Weberian notion of bureaucracy or the traditional management theory of organization which does not view the individual as active agent but a reactive unity to be homogenized. For example, we found no way to define the new types of organizations being designed that have focussed on increasing the individual's 'return' on his investment in the organization. Also, the appropriate-fit notions of Perrow, Thompson, Burns and others have apparently ignored the possibility that an organic system may be useful in the setting that they now consider to be appropriate for a mechanistic system. All the theories are therefore conservative, especially in the direction of enhancing the quality of the individual life within a complex organization.

The point may also be illustrated in the study of other problems, for example, poverty. 'Descriptive studies uninfluenced by some commitment to their problems are worse than useless; they are an implied threat to the poor... Even an effort to see and present all sides constitutes a bias since it implicitly supports the *status quo* (Padfield 1970, pp. 34–5). The writer even goes as far as suggesting that the culture of poverty theses 'will die a hard death... [partly] because the scientific establishment has an investment in it' (p. 35). Goering notes that much of social science research supports the existing power system (Goering 1970, p. 51).

This essentially conservative appropriate-fit posture misses a critical attribute of people in power who strive to be innovative. The fundamental assumption that these people make is that there are no independent variables; that through various actions, it is their task to make what they wish come true (i.e. to make self-fulfilling prophecies). These men prefer theories that do not focus on the *status quo* and that ignore the dynamics of individual and small group processes. Perhaps this is one reason why organizational sociologists have a 'perennial problem ... of gaining access to organizations' (Smelser and Davis 1969, p. 66).

DILEMMAS AND TENSIONS IN DEFINING NORMATIVE VIEWS: AN EXAMPLE FROM ORGANIZATIONAL THEORY

Earlier we stated that society may justifiably (in its eyes) limit the conduct of research and inquiry that violates its values and goes beyond its present limits of appropriateness. Now we have stated that researchers have an obligation to design new concepts of man and organizations that go beyond the present limits of appropriateness. How is this dilemma and tension to be dealt with?

(1) Some scholars select those values that they prefer and build their case around those values. The difficulty with this approach is that scholarship based upon personal preferences can easily become an ideology. The view may no longer be testable or tested. Once this occurs holding such a position would tend to violate the values of valid information, free and informed choice, and internal commitment to that choice. The violation of these values, in turn, would tend to lead to the Orwellian 1984 where some experts are in control defining our alternatives and preferences.

(2) Another alternative is to conduct inquiries about basic values and focus on those that seem basic to all or most cultures. This approach assumes that there is some validity to values that stand the test of time in settings where life is viewed in significantly different ways. The strength of this approach is that it is basically one of trying to identify values that are selected by a wide variance of people and cultures. Such an approach may more easily resist becoming an ideology since by its very emphasis on comparative studies it assumes inquiry is worth while and some form of empirical validation necessary. The difficulty with this approach is that the results could be an amalgamation of what would fit in the 'average' or in the model society but have questionable meaning for a given case.

(3) A third alternative would be to select those values that seem basic to many cultures, identify their functional and dysfunctional

aspects, then help a given society design the type of world in which it wishes to live. In our case, scholars may be asked to help the society decide what it will define as the basic qualities of life and then help its members to design and manage organizations which enhance the quality of life *and* assure that the organizations can survive and produce the outputs (in the form of services or materials) that the society values.

How does one go about defining some of the values that imply a high quality of life? One possibility is to design a world in which the members are able to actualize more effectively the potential endemic in human beings. What is this human potential?

One way to identify human potentialities is to seek those descriptive qualities of man that also represent his potentialities. For example, two legs are a descriptive 'given' of man. We may then say that in order to walk man should place one foot first and then the second foot (or define some way the legs are to be used). The *ought* is therefore derivable from the *is*.

In our area of interest one can explore the literature from anthropology, psychology and sociology to identify any qualities of human nature that exist in many different cultures. Once these are identified one may then ask what kinds of systems would be created if these qualities were to be valued (as highly as the survival of the system).

After an examination of the personality literature, it was concluded that scholars agreed encouragingly on describing how, or along what dimensions, human personality developed (presumably because personality development was empirically observable). There was significantly less agreement on how to explain human personality and its development.

The writer chose to develop a model that described personality development instead of selecting a particular theory of personality. Such a tactic would hopefully minimize the value judgments implicit in the various personality theories. One way to identify the requirements of human personality would be to identify the development trends. One could then hypothesize that the requirements of human personality would be to fulfill these trends.

The properties that were inferred from the literature and conceptualized as seven personality trends were identified (briefly) as the individual, in our society, tended to develop from (1) passivity to an increasing state of activity, (2) from dependence to a state of relative independence (interdependence), (3) from behaving in a few ways as an infant to developing capability of behaving in many different ways as an adult, (4) from having erratic, casual, shallow, quickly-dropped interests to having deeper, longer lasting interests, (5) from holding a short-time perspective to a longer time perspective, (6) from being in a subordinate position in the family and society to a more equal or superordinate position relative to their peers, and (7) from a lack of awareness of self to an awareness and control over self (Argyris 1957, pp. 49–53).

It is important to point out that these are dimensions that purport to represent a model of the dynamics and potentialities of human development. As a model, these dimensions say *nothing* about (1) the writer's preferences as to whether individuals should or ought to develop in these directions or (2) the empirical frequencies with which individuals develop in these directions. However, the model could be used to conduct empirical research where an individual could be studied in terms of these dimensions and be located empirically on each dimension. Thus individual differences or social class differences could be identified.

Once the requirements of human potentiality were defined, the next step was to compare them with the potential requirements of formal organization. The assumption was that much could be learned about organizations by understanding how each of these organic unities interacted with, indeed transacted upon, the other. For example, specific *a priori* predictions could be made about human behavior in organizations if we knew the degree to which the participants felt their needs were being frustrated or facilitated by organizational requirements. A simple theoretical analysis showed that there were two conditions under which human needs could be frustrated. They were:

if the individual aspired	and	*if the organization required that*
(1) toward the 'adult' ends of the seven continua or trends		(1) the individuals worked in highly specialized, molecularized work and in positions with minimal power and administrative control.
(2) toward the 'infant' ends of the seven continua or trends		(2) the individuals worked in challenging, enlarged jobs with power and control over their immediate work world.

Under *either* of these two conditions one could derive that the employees would tend to be frustrated, in conflict, and would adapt by creating informal activities ranging from trade unions to apathy, to physical and psychological withdrawal, to developing a market orientation or instrumental attitudes (Argyris 1957).

It was further hypothesized, still remaining at the level of derivations from a theoretical framework, that the informal activities listed above should *not* tend to appear if there was a fit between the individual's needs and the organization's requirements. This would tend to occur:

if the individuals aspired	and	*the organization required that*
(3) toward the 'adult' ends of the continua		(3) the individuals worked under 'adult' conditions listed in (2)
(4) toward the 'infant' ends of the continua		(4) the individuals worked under 'infant' conditions listed in (1)

Up to this point we have been operating at the theoretical level of analysis. Nothing has been said about where any given individual or group of individuals actually stands on these personality dimensions or the requirements made of them by their respective jobs. Nor have we said anything about the concepts of minimum development or about preferred development. All we have is a model composed of dimensions which can be used to construct individual need and job requirement profiles for purposes of comparing the degree of expression that is possible as job requirements interact with the need requirements.

Next, we took a leap toward empirical reality and hypothesized that the predominant conditions in 'real' life between personality and organization was (1). The next step was to see if any research existed which described the conditions under (1) and which supported the existence of the consequences derivable from such a state of affairs. Much research was found to illustrate both of these types of data (Argyris 1957, 1964).

Were there any studies that did not support the predictions of the first state of affairs? There were several *and* these were shown to fit under the other theoretically derived but empirically infrequent conditions. For example, the writer published studies of several organizations where the employees preferred work composed of the 'infant' ends of the continua and the organization offered them such work (condition (4)). It was shown, as predicted, that the informal activities of trade unionism, hostility toward management, absenteeism, turnover, hardly existed (Argyris 1960).

All the studies recently cited by Strauss (1970) as evidence against the personality-and-organization view actually confirm it.

For example Vroom found that people who have a high need for independence and weak authoritarian attitudes would prefer to work with 'adult' conditions. This would be predictable from the personality-and-organization framework. In terms of our model above they would fit under conditions (3). The same may be said for McClelland's and Atkinson's findings that people with high 'need achievement' react well to jobs with 'adult' requirements while those who are low prefer the less challenging and safe jobs (in our terms jobs that fit the infant ends of our continua). Turner's and Lawrence's and Hulin's and Blood's studies that rural workers prefer work approximating the more adult ends of our continua were explained by the former on religious grounds. Strauss, Hulin and Blood question this interpretation, as does the writer. There is no evidence to suggest that Catholic workers are not as involved in their work as are Protestant workers. Hulin and Blood explained the differences by postulating that the rural workers adhere to the Protestant ethic of achievement while urban workers look upon the job merely as a means of obtaining satisfactions off the job (Strauss 1970, p. 155).

The writer's explanation would be consonant with part of Hulin's and Blood's explanation, if we may assume that the operational definition of the Protestant ethic is consonant with the adult ends of the continua (e.g. seeking challenge, opportunity to express one's abilities etc.). If so, then our explanation has several advantages. First, there is no need to add a new concept to explain the findings. Moreover, the concept (Protestant ethic) is not, as yet, an integral part of a social science theoretical framework presented by scholars attempting to understand these phenomena. Hulin and Blood selected it presumably because it fitted their hypothesis about the causal relationships. More importantly, however, our framework, without adding new concepts and processes, can be used to explain certain dynamics in workers' attitudes that the Hulin and Blood explanation does not explain. It has been shown that rural workers soon take on the attitudes of urban workers after decades of work in the plant even though the community has not become significantly more urbanized (Argyris 1960). How would Hulin and Blood explain such data? Would they not have to hypothesize that the rural employees lost their Protestant ethic? If so, what is the process by which this occurs? Our theory would suggest the following dynamics.

People brought up in a rural area live in a world closer to condition (3). They enter a plant and, in the early stages where organizations are being built and are growing, there is enough flexibility in jobs and in control systems for continued expression of the 'adult' ends of the continua. As the growth of the plant levels off, and it becomes increasingly managerially tight and controlled, the organization begins to require the employee to perform in a work world closer to condition (1). Soon the employees (who are still rural) begin to act just as their urban brethren have been doing for years because the conditions inside the plant are more like the conditions inside the older plants in cities. Moreover both sets may teach their children not to get involved in their work. 'Get your money and get the hell out.' Thus, although our hypothesis is that the process of change begins with the change inside the organization, we note that this change is taken outside to the culture. It influences both the socio-cultural norms and institutions as well as the socialization of the young. The latter are taught not to become too involved in work; they are encouraged to take on an instrumental attitude. A feedback loop is therefore formed from the plant to the environment and back into the plant.

If the causal factors were in the environment (as Turner and Lawrence suggest) or the Protestant ethic (Hulin and Blood) then how would these views explain the work of Banks (1960) and Mann and Williams (1962)? The former found that workers reported higher job satisfaction after their work was redesigned to have more variety and responsibility (Banks 1960, pp. 24–5). The latter reported similar results although they carefully documented an increase in employee internal tension. Also how would one explain the increased employee involvement, productivity, and satisfaction on the parts of employees whose work has been genuinely enlarged through participation in Scanlon Plan activities (Shultz and Cresara 1952); and job enrichment (Ford 1969, Myers 1968)? In all these cases, the workers did not, as far as can be ascertained, seek to or actually alter their address, religion, nor was their Protestant ethic affected.[1]

[1] Nor does the study by Whyte cited by Strauss necessarily disconfirm the theory. It may be that Peruvians are brought up to accept a greater degree of dependence and to expect less utilization of their abilities. Under those conditions, close supervision would be predictably positively correlated with job satisfaction (as reported by Whyte).

Another criticism levelled against the personality-and-organization approach may be illustrated by Gross' recent work (1970). He states that the organization approach exaggerates the degree of employee dissatisfaction. He notes that, in most published studies, less than 15% of the workers tend to express dissatisfaction with their work.

First, the personality-and-organization approach does not seek to make predictions about the dissatisfaction employees experience – if dissatisfaction operationally means responding to such a question as how satisfied or dissatisfied the respondent feels about his job. The theory makes predictions about such variables as the individual's desire to express his abilities, to have control over his immediate work world etc. Argyris has cited research by such scholars as Kahn and Weiss, Blauner, Kornhauser, and Inkeles that show that desire for autonomy and control over one's work world is a strong and deep-seated motive and that this need tends to increase as one goes up the organizational hierarchy (or occupational ladder) (Argyris 1964, pp. 50–7). Recently Tannenbaum has replicated these findings in two hundred organizational units (Tannenbaum 1968) and Zupanov and Tannenbaum (1968) reported similar results in studies of Yugoslavian plants.

The report of job satisfaction on a questionnaire does not, therefore, necessarily test condition (1) above, which is the one the critics have focussed on. Satisfaction (as typically measured) could exist under conditions (3) and (4). It could also exist under conditions (1) and (2), *if* such things as job security, a strong informal system and a strong union exist.

Beyond these issues, there is another argument that must not be ignored. What does it mean to assert that workers are satisfied to choose dull, boring jobs and to seek non-involvement? How does one arrive at that conclusion? In order to answer the question, we begin by noting that the assertion is based upon the empirically documented fact that respectable correlations between molecularized work and job satisfaction have been found (Hulin and Blood). But what does correlation mean? It could mean what Hulin and Blood imply, namely that workers are genuinely satisfied with their present work. But satisfaction with one's world can be influenced by the perceived degree to which the world is considered alterable. Most of the correlations reported occur under conditions where workers know that there is little probability of other types of work.

Could it be that one way for the workers to reduce their dissonance and frustration would be to accept the present restrictions and to decide that their happiness should be within the existing power structure? The strategy may make sense to them because to aspire actively to the impossible is asking for psychological frustration.

A statement by behavioral scientists that the individual worker should be permitted to remain at work in a job providing, it is said, job satisfaction *because* the reported job satisfaction means that the worker has freely chosen and prefers that state of affairs to others is a *normative* and *untested* position. This position assumes that because the employee is satisfied, he actively prefers to remain on the job and that the process by which he chose to remain permitted him to explore other attractive possibilities. There is actually little evidence that such choice processes do exist. Workers may have a choice but the range of jobs open to blue collar workers (in terms of complexity, innovation, degree of control) is not very large. For example, it has been reported that 90% of the jobs open to blue collar workers in Detroit could be learned in a week or less.

Behavioral scientists have documented that a person's sense of satisfaction is partially determined by what is available (relative deprivation) and by the norms of peer reference groups. Thus the worker is faced with a world in which there is not much variance in work; where the peer or reference group norms are away from job involvement and more toward a market orientation.

Thus when Goldthorpe *et al.* (1969) and Walker and Guest (1952, p. 91) report that workers leave jobs that are perceived by them to be more intrinsically satisfying and go to jobs that are less so but pay more, this does not necessarily prove that workers do not prefer intrinsic work. Four other possible explanations are that (1) the degree of intrinsic satisfaction is not very high in *any* job available to them, (2) the employees are concentrating on fulfillment of the basic psychological and security needs, (3) the employees have chosen the market-orientation and thus they look elsewhere for intrinsic satisfaction, and (4) the fulfillment of needs for variety, challenging work etc. is only one set of factors that are related to intrinsic satisfaction at work. The leadership style of the supervisors, the administrative controls such as budgets, production bogeys, and quality control may be more powerful to cause the employee to leave than the intrinsic job satisfaction can cause him to remain. If supervisors are not very effective and if administrative controls are very controlling and arbitrary, then the intrinsic satisfactions from the job could be negated – hence leaving to go to a job which pays more money makes good sense to the employee.

Therefore when behavioral scientists decide to take presently existing states of affairs as the ones they would support, because employees state that they are satisfied, they ought to be aware that this means they opt for the *status quo*. As we have suggested Strauss does this at the individual level (Argyris 1968), Burns and Stalker, Lawrence and Lorsch at the organizational level.

Another frequent argument that implies value judgments and changes the researcher's role from the descriptive 'neutral' to the 'normative' one of opting for the *status quo* is illustrated by the argument that many workers do not prefer to actualize themselves (in the direction of intrinsic needs). Actualization, the critics maintain, is a middle class value, one that academics prefer and actually project on to the worker. Elsewhere, the writer has presented evidence that self-actualization, as defined by these seven continua, is understood and desired by *all* classes (Argyris 1964). Indeed, the interview material in Goldthorpe *et al.* and the Kohn data, cited in this book, support this view for lower level employees.

Gross (1970) and Strauss (1963) have taken this position. To quote from a more recent study, Gross suggests that concepts like 'individual dignity', 'self-development' probably represent academic values more than employee desires because employees very rarely report the need to express such values. Even if we were to agree with Gross (and there is ample evidence in the history of the labor movement and its demands to question his view) the problem is whether this state of affairs implies that people ought to accept them and indeed ought to be trained to adapt to them? Gross seems to suggest that this should be the case. He states that there is little one could do to provide opportunities for self-actualization and indeed it might frighten some people if they were offered such opportunities. Moreover, he notes that assembly-line jobs do not require a worker who demonstrates initiative, who desires variety. 'One wants him [the worker] simply to work according to an established pace. Creativity, then, is not always desirable' (Gross 1970, p. 103).

Note the logic. Gross begins by stating that the personality-and-organizations cannot state that one *should* (italics his) provide workers with more challenge or autonomy in accordance with their values because to do so would be to rest their case, not on a scientific theory (which describes what is – not what ought to be) but a program for organizations. Then he suggests that no one has proven how harmful are dissatisfaction, anxiety, dependency, and conformity to the individual (which is probably correct). He continues to say that a certain amount of these conditions is unavoidable and necessary and helpful (and he provides no empirical data for this assertion). Then Gross concludes that employees should be educated to live within this world.

> Perhaps the most general conclusion we can draw is that since organizations appear to be inevitable . . . a major type of socialization of the young ought to include methods for dealing with the organization . . . [For example] an important consideration in the preparation of individuals for work should include training for the handling of or adjustment to authority (Gross 1970, pp. 104–5).

At this point Gross has taken a normative position. And again we see an example of how what *is* at time T_1 becomes what *ought to be* if it is to be continued at time T_2. Descriptive theories about the present state of the universe inevitably become normative if someone suggests or assumes that they are or should continue to exist. Once having made this assumption, as in the case of Gross, socialization to the present state of affairs follows logically.

The quarrel with Gross is therefore on his apparent unwillingness to see that behavioral scientists *are* being normative whenever they make statements about how individuals should adapt to the present state of the universe; to his apparent disinterest in recommending further research on how to redesign organizations, jobs, administrative controls, and leadership; to his implicit strategy that change in our universe should come from others than the behavioral scientists who should act as rigorous scribes of reality.

It is our position that behavioral scientists have a valuable service to perform in thinking through normative models of the world, testing them as rigorously as possible, and offering the knowledge to our society. For example, the author prefers to develop new organizational forms where dependence, use of few abilities, psychological failure are de-emphasized; where there are greater opportunities for openness, trust, and risk-taking for several reasons. Developing new types of organizations provides the scientist with new opportunities to study a greater variance in organizations. This variance should provide new insights as well as increased opportunities to test hypotheses. Thus the scientific base for generalizations is enlarged and the opportunity to disconfirm or confirm theories increased.

The second reason is based upon the assumption that the areas where individual self-expression and organizational effectiveness support and reinforce one another have not been studied sufficiently. I believe there are many more possibilities than are presently envisioned where individual actualization and organizational effectiveness can benefit each other. As these opportunities become known and utilized the participants may also become more open to systematic studies of the conditions under which the individual's actualization may need to give in to the organization's requirements for effectiveness and vice versa. It is my belief that individuals will permit and encourage the organization's need to be met at a cost to them if they believe their opportunities for actualization are as high as it is possible to design without harming the organization and if they can see the need for, and therefore experience as legitimate, certain organizational demands that may act to ignore or indeed frustrate their needs. I value enhanced opportunities for individuals to increase their self-esteem, confidence, and learning because I consider such attributes as positive contributors to the quality of life *and* because organizations populated with individuals with such qualities have a higher probability of overcoming what John Gardner has aptly called 'organizational dry rot' and what I have called 'organizational entropy'. It will be such organizations that will tend to provide higher quality services and products at lower human and material costs.

I believe, therefore, that our society has an obligation to design organizations that may require more initiative, creativity and involvement. I also believe that such organizations have a right to require such behavior of individuals. Moreover, as behavioral scientists generate such knowledge, they should also generate knowledge about how individuals and organizations can productively confront each other (which would include dealing openly with and maintaining productive conflict). Recently, I have attempted to develop the foundations for a theory of intervention where the interventionist strives to help all the individuals enlarge their degree of free and informed choice. To put this another way, behavioral scientists increase their freedom to design new organizations as they also design processes by which individuals are strengthened to confront and reject these organizations (Argyris 1970).

THE INDIVIDUAL AND THE SYSTEM

One of the basic questions raised at the outset was whether the social system could be profitably viewed as autonomous from the individuals in it. Blau, Thompson and Perrow, it appears, would reply affirmatively, whereas Goldthorpe and Lockwood would reply negatively but then create a theory that has such unintended consequences. This analysis leads not only to inconsistent and incomplete sociology, but it also leads to difficulties when one considers creating changes in ongoing systems.

Individuals and social systems are independent of each other in trivial ways. Certainly it is true that any given individual may come and go, but the system exists. The system will exist *as long as* the individuals in it behave according to its requirements. In other words systems require that individuals behave according to certain prescribed roles. When they do, sociologists apparently conclude that the system tends to be autonomous from the individuals. Why do they conclude this? I assume because when they observe the actual behavior, they see that it conforms to role requirements and roles are part of the system.

There are, at least, two difficulties involved in this logic. First, we may recall that individuals in formal organizations (especially at the lower levels) are typically asked to take on roles which exclude many of their properties as human beings. They acquiesce partly because they have to if they are to earn a living and partly because they eventually take on a market-orientation and psychologically withdraw from work. But a role of psychological withdrawal is hard work and consumes people's energy as well as reducing the amount they are willing to give to work. There is much psychological activity that goes unnoticed by the sociologist as he focusses primarily on the observable fact that role requirements are being carried on.

The second and more powerful way in which the continuous connection between individual and system can be seen is when one attempts to create change in the system. One soon finds that in ignoring individuals and, for example, changing structures unilaterally, one operates within an authoritarian intervention posture that not only decreases free choice and increases resistance but also increases the probability that the behavioral scientist will not continue to obtain valid data from his informants. Thus unilateral change not only runs the risk of harming people (especially those with little power), it also runs the risk of making research data less valid and research activity less valued by the people in the society, who are the subjects upon which we depend.

This does not mean that no changes can be brought about by changing the structure or that all changes must begin with interpersonal relationships. Next, let us consider a model that sheds some light on selecting the appropriate sequences in organizational change.

SEQUENCES IN ORGANIZATIONAL CHANGE

Elsewhere it has been suggested that organizational structure, technology and administrative control systems tend to place the lower level participants in a dependent submissive relationship with little control over their work situation, where they use a few of their abilities and are exposed to continual psychological failure. At the upper levels the participants find themselves in intra- and intergroup conflicts, competing for scarce resources in a managerial climate dominated by conformity, mistrust, and organizational defensiveness etc.

What kinds of intervention strategies may be used under these conditions? In attempting to answer this question, let us assume that the interventionist strives to use strategies that (1) decrease the restraining forces of change, (2) decrease dysfunctionality and organizational pressures, (3) increase the probability of getting valid information, and developing conditions for informal choice and internal commitment, which should lead (4) to an increase in the probability that the clients can remain autonomous from the interventionists and in control of their system. According to our analysis any intervention activity that placed individuals in the same kinds of situations already being created by formal organizations will tend to fail in terms of these four criteria. The hypothesis is that change strategies based upon 'mechanistic organization' or 'theory X' (concepts admittedly oversimplified) will tend to fail in terms of the four criteria defined above.

The reasons why failure is predicted might be illustrated by figure 4. We note five dimensions depicting conditions for effective change. Present formal organizations tend to create conditions that are away from those that have been shown to be relevant for increasing system competence. For example, trust, openness, and risk taking are rare in formal organizations, and deviate significantly from the mistrust, closedness, and emphasis on stability which we suggest are more typical. Thus the behavior that may be necessary for effective change and for continued system competence deviates significantly from the existing norms (dimension I). We may therefore hypothesize that the degree of unfreezing required in the client system (II) will also be high. There will also be a strong necessity for the creation of self-corrective mechanisms (III) with the involvement of all the relevant clients (IV) which should suggest (during the change period) a high degree of personal and system discomfort (V). The higher the change programs score on all these dimensions the more difficult they will tend to be, for the clients and the interventionist, to plan, to execute and to monitor.

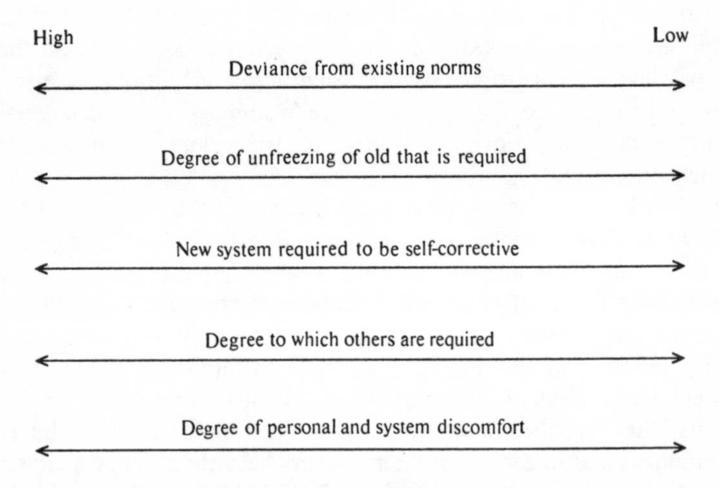

Figure 4. Conditions for effective change

The more difficult the change program, the more client internal commitment is necessary if they are to be effective. The more internal commitment that is necessary, the more the clients need to be involved in the design, execution and monitoring of the changes. However, such client involvement, if it is to be helpful, requires clients who are, among other things, open, experimental, risk taking, high in trust. But these are the qualities that the formal systems tend to lack. These states of affairs cannot, in the writer's opinion, be created without focussing upon the interpersonal relations and group dynamics of the top group in particular. As the relationships at the top become more effective, then the client system will be in a more advantageous position to design, execute and monitor its own changes in structure, power, reward systems etc. (with the assistance of the interventionist). Unless these relationships become more effective, it is questionable how much long lasting effective change will be possible. This is true, we suggest, even if the changes contemplated are in the work environment at the lower levels. For example, Professors Edward Lawler and Richard Hackman have recently conducted a study of job enlargement. They have presented evidence that for job enlargement to be effective in the long run the leadership styles of the first to middle levels of management may have to change. Moreover, the budgetary and production control systems may need to be redesigned.[1] Neither type of change seems likely without changes in top management behavior and policy. Unless top management is committed to the behavioral and policy implications of changes at lower levels, they may intentionally or unintentionally subvert progress when it becomes threatening.

Argyris (1960) and Bennis (1966) have cited similar examples and have shown that employees at the lower level may suffer more from these unilateral changes than those at the upper levels and that progress toward change can be seriously inhibited. If one begins at the top the disequilibrium at the lower levels caused by unilateral top management withdrawals or reversals is minimized. On the other hand, if interventions are begun at the top, and if the top management's internal commitment is high, they can become the effective 'change agents' within their own organization and facilitate effective change.

A question frequently asked is why may not an interventionist intervene directly to make changes by, for example, altering the structure or technology. A definitive answer requires research that is as yet unavailable. However, several reasons might be cited for

[1] Personal communication. Professors Lawler and Hackman may be contacted at the Department of Administrative Sciences, Yale University.

the sake of this discussion (and they may also serve as hypotheses for such research). First, how does one make direct changes without becoming unilateral in the use of power and thereby limiting the client's free choice and internal commitment? Can unilateral action be taken without reducing the clients' system's free choice and internal commitment?

Secondly, is the available systematic knowledge about organizations adequate to be the basis of action taken directly by a consultant? Is it not true that the design of new organizational structures or administrative control systems, for example, still requires a long process of experimentation before the correct solution can be found? If so, then is it not necessary to have the full internal commitment of the client system if the changes are to be effectively monitored and continuously modified?

Some may cite such changes as those reported by Whyte and Hamilton (1964), by Trist and his colleagues (1962) and by Blau and Scott (1968) where the environment was altered directly without focussing on interpersonal relationships. One way to explain the success of these ventures (in the case of Whyte and Hamilton, Blau and Scott) is that neither of their innovations (introducing a water spigot in the coffee dining shop or developing a new procedural manual) required the learning of significantly new and deviant behavior; therefore the unfreezing required was not high, the self-correcting mechanisms necessary were not of major consequence and personal or system discomfort was not high. In sum, these are changes that would tend to fall on the low end of our continua. Under these conditions we would predict that direct environmental change would be relatively well accepted with minimal need for work in the interpersonal and group area. The same may be said for the changes that Trist designed for the coal miners. The social system that was designed fitted the men's needs and the technical system.

Recently several case studies have been published of top management groups that attempted to introduce structural changes before they altered the degree of openness, risk taking, and experimenting in their interpersonal and group dynamics. The data suggest that the structural changes were neither fully developed nor effectively introduced. One of the biggest bottlenecks was the interpersonal and group dynamics of the top groups. Their dynamics led to members having their ideas about structural changes undercut, little additiveness in the discussions about organizational change, therefore leading to minimal sense of clarity or agreement with understandably less internal commitment to any given structural change (Argyris 1971a).

It is experiences such as these that lead the writer to suggest that the processes for effective change should begin at the top with the interpersonal and group dynamics. As these become more effective there is a higher probability that genuine and underlying organizational changes will be considered by the clients, carefully explored and effectively maintained.

Even though the contrary has been repeatedly emphasized, the focus on interpersonal relations and the expression of feelings has been interpreted by some to mean that rationality should be substituted by emotionality, and interpersonal competence for technical competence. Nothing could be further from our intent. Whyte writes:

> A close reading of some of Argyris' writings suggests that his position has sometimes been caricatured . . . The Argyris prescription . . . is not a substitution of emotionalism for technical, rational discussion. He advocates what he calls 'openness' or 'authenticity', which is his particular combination of rational *and* emotional communication. Openness does not mean that each individual should express whatever is on his mind regardless of any concern for the feelings of others. The aim is to create a situation in which the members of an organization who are working closely together can each express how they feel about problems in their relationships in such a manner as to help those with whom they are communicating to express themselves in a similar open manner. The theory is that the emotional problems within the group do not simply disappear when they are not faced by members of the group; rather they tend to obstruct the carrying out of the rational plans of the members (Whyte 1970).

To summarize, the more the change programs require behavioral changes that tend to be high on the five continua, the more it will be necessary to focus first on interpersonal and group factors. The closer the changes fall on the low ends of the continua, the more one can go directly to environmental changes.

REFERENCES

Aiken, M., and Hage, J. 'Organizational interdependence and intra-organizational structure', *American Journal of Sociology*, 1968, 33(6), 912–31.

Alderfer, C. P. 'The organizational syndrome', *Administrative Science Quarterly*, 1967, 12, 440–60.

Allen, S. A., III. 'Corporate-divisional relationships in highly diversified forms'. In J. Lorsch and P. Lawrence (eds.), *Studies in organizational design*, Homewood, Ill., R. D. Irwin, 1970, pp. 16–35.

Allport, G. 'Normative compatibility in the light of social science'. In A. Maslow (ed.), *New knowledge in human values*, New York, Harper, 1960, pp. 137–50.

Angyal, A. *Foundations for a science of personality*, New York, Commonwealth Fund, 1941.

Arensberg, C., and McGregor, D. 'Determination of morale in an industrial company', *Applied Anthropology*, 1942, 1, 12–34.

Argyris, C. *Management and organizational development*, New York, McGraw-Hill, 1971*a*.

'Problems and new directions for industrial psychology'. In M. Dunnette (ed.), *Handbook of industrial and organizational psychology*, Chicago, Rand McNally, 1971*b*.

Intervention theory and method, Reading, Mass., Addison-Wesley, 1970*a*.

'Management information systems: The challenge to rationality and emotionality', *Management Science*, 1970*b*.

'The incompleteness of social psychological theory', *American Psychologist*, 1969, 24(10), 893–908.

'Some unintended consequences of rigorous research', *Psychological Bulletin*, 1968, 70, 185–97.

Some causes of organizational ineffectiveness within the Department of State, Center for International Systems Research, Department of State, 1967.

Organization and innovation, Homewood, Ill., R. D. Irwin, 1965.

Integrating the individual and the organization, New York, Wiley, 1964.

Understanding organizational behavior. Homewood, Ill., Dorsey Press, 1960.

Diagnosing human relations in organizations; a case study of a hospital, New Haven, Labor and Management Center, Yale University, 1956.

Personality and organization, New York, Harper Bros., 1957.

Organization of a bank, Labor and Management Center, Yale University, 1954.

Banks, O. *The attitudes of steelworkers to technological change*, Liverpool University Press, 1960.

Barker, R., and Wright, H. *Midwest and its children*, Evanston, Ill., Row-Peterson, 1955.

Bennis, W. *Changing organizations*, New York, McGraw-Hill, 1966.

Benoit-Guilbat, O. 'The sociology of work'. In D. L. Sills (ed.), *International Encyclopedia of Social Sciences*, New York, Macmillan, 1968, 7, 230–40.

Blake, R. R., Shepard, H. A., and Mouton, J. S. *Managing inter-group conflict in industry*, Houston, Gulf Publishing, 1964.

Blau, P. M. 'A formal theory of differentiation in organizations', *American Sociological Review*, 1970a, 35(2), 201–18.

'Decentralization in bureaucracies'. In M. N. Zald (ed.), *Power in organizations*, Nashville, Tenn., Vanderbilt University Press, 1970*b*.

'Theories of organizations', *International Encyclopedia of Social Sciences*, New York, Macmillan, 1968, 2, 297–304.

'Comparative study of organizations', *Industrial and Labor Relations Review*, 1965, 18(3), 323–38.

Blau, P. M., and Schoenherr, R. A., with the collaboration of Klatzry, S. R. 'The structure of organizations', manuscript, in press, 1970.

Blau, P. M., and Scott, W. *Formal organizations*, San Francisco, Chandler, 1968.

Blauner, R. *Alienation and freedom*, Chicago, University of Chicago Press, 1964.

Boulding, K. 'Economics as a moral science', *American Economic Review*, 1969, 59(1). 1–12.

Bower, J. L. 'Planning within the firm', *American Economic Review*, 1970, 60(2), 186–94.
Braun, A. C. 'On the origin of cancer cells', *American Scientist*, 1970, 58(3), 307–20.
Bruner, J. S. *The relevance of education*, W. W. Norton, 1971.
Bugental, J. *The search for authenticity*, New York, Holt, Rinehart and Winston, 1965.
Burns, T., and Stalker, G. *The management of innovation*, London, Tavistock Publications, 1961.
Campbell, D. T. 'Ethnocentricism of disciplines and the fish-scale model of omniscience'. In M. and C. Sherif (eds.), *Interdisciplinary relationships in the social sciences*, Chicago, Aldine Publishing Co., 1969, 328–48.
Chandler, A. D., Jr. *Strategy and structure*, Cambridge, Mass., M.I.T. Press, 1962.
Coleman, J. *The adolescent society*, New York, Glencoe Free Press, 1961.
Cronbach, L. G., and Gleser, J. C. *Psychological tests and personnel decisions*, University of Illinois Press, 1965.
Cyert, R. M., and March, J. G. *A behavioral theory of the firm*, Englewood Cliffs, N.J., Prentice-Hall, 1963.
DeCharms, R. *Personal causation*, New York, Academic Press, 1968.
Denzin, N. K. 'Who leads: Sociology or society?' *The American Sociologist*, 1970, 4(2), 125–7.
Dunnington, R. A. 'Research for organization theory and management action: Introduction', Sixteenth Annual Meeting, Industrial Relations Research Association, December 1963, 1–5.
Etzioni, A. *The active society*, 1969.
Modern organizations, Englewood Cliffs, N.J., Prentice-Hall, 1964.
A comparative analysis of complex organizations, Glencoe, Ill., The Free Press, 1961.
Etzkowitz, H. 'Institution formation sociology', *American Sociologist*, 1970, 5(2), 120–4.
Feinstein, A. R. *Clinical judgment*, Baltimore, Williams and Wilkins, 1967.
Ford, R. N. *Motivation through the work itself*, American Management Association, 1969.
Fromm, E. *The sane society*, New York, Rinehart, 1955.

Gardner, J. 'America in the twenty-third century', *New York Times* (editorial page), 27 July 1968.

Goldthorpe, J. H. 'Social inequality and social integration in modern Britain', British Association for the Advancement of Science: Presidential address, September 1969 (mimeographed, King's College, Cambridge).

'Images of class among affluent workers', Department of Applied Economics, University of Cambridge, mimeographed, n.d.

Goldthorpe, J. H., Lockwood, D. L., Bechofer, F., and Platt, J. *The affluent worker: industrial attitudes and behavior*, New York, Cambridge University Press, 1969.

Goering, J. M. 'Intervention research and the survey process', *Journal of Social Issues*, 1970, 26(4), 49–55.

Gooding, J. 'It pays to wake up to the blue-collar worker', *Fortune*, 1970 (September), 133–5.

Goodman, R. A. 'Review of *The Theory of Organization*', *British Journal of Industrial Relations*, March 1971, 9(1), 132–4.

Gouldner, A. 'Organizational analyses'. In R. K. Merton and L. Broom, Jr. (eds.), *Sociology today*, New York, Basic Books, 1959.

Patterns of industrial bureaucracy, Glencoe, Ill., The Free Press, 1954.

Greiner, L. E., Leitch, D. P., and Barnes, L. B. 'The simple complexity of organizational climate in a government agency'. In R. Taguiri and G. H. Litwin (eds.). *Organizational climate*, Harvard University, Graduate School of Business, 1968, 152–221.

Gross, E. 'Work, organization and stress'. In S. Levine and N. Scotch (eds.), *Social Stress*, Chicago, Aldine Publishing Co., 1970, 54–110.

Guest, R. *Organizational change*, Homewood, Ill., Dorsey Press, 1962.

Hage, J., and Aiken, M. *Social change in complex organizations*, New York, Random House, 1970.

'Routine technology, social structure and organization goals', *Administrative Science Quarterly*, 1969, 14(3), 366–77.

Hall, C. S., and Lindzey, G. *Theories of personality*, New York, Wiley, 1957.

Hall, D. T., and Lawler, E. E. 'Attitude and behavior patterns in research and development organizations', sponsored by the Connecticut Research Commission and Department of Administrative Sciences, May 1968.

Hall, R. H. 'The concept of bureaucracy: An empirical assessment', *American Journal of Sociology*, 1963, 69(1), 32–40.

Heilbroner, R. L. 'On the limited "relevance" of economics', *Public Interest*, Fall, 1970, 21, 80–93.

Hewitt, J. P. *Social stratification and deviant behavior*. New York, Random House, 1970.

Hickson, D. J., Pugh, D. S., and Pheipey, C. 'Operations technology and organization structure: An empirical reappraisal', *Administrative Science Quarterly*, 1969, 14(3), 378–97.

Holmberg, A. 'Participant intervention in the field', *Human Organization*, Spring, 1955, 14, 23–6.

Holt, R. R. 'Yet another look at clinical and statistical prediction: is clinical psychology worthwhile?' *American Psychologist*, 1970, 25(4), 337–49.

Homans, G. C. *The nature of social science*, New York, Harcourt, Brace and World, 1967.

'Bringing men back in', *American Sociological Review*, 1964, 29, 809–18.

Hoopes, T. *The limits of intervention*, New York, David McKay, 1969.

Ingham, G. 'Organizational size, orientation to work, and industrial behavior', *Sociology*, 1967, 1, 239–58.

Iris, B., and Barrett, G. W. 'Effect of job attitudes upon satisfaction with life', Technical Report 38, Management Research Center, The Graduate School of Management, University of Rochester, 1970.

Jahoda, M. *Positive mental health*, New York, Basic Books, 1958.

Jameson, J., and Hessler, R. M. 'The natives are restless: the ethos and mythos of student power', *Human Organization*, 1970, 20(2), 81–94.

Jaques, E. 'Two contributions to a general theory of organization and management', *Scientific Business*, August 1964, 1–12.

Kaufman, H., and Seidman, D. 'The morphology of organizations', *Administrative Science Quarterly*, 1970, 15(4), 439–52.

Kelman, H. C. *A time to speak*, San Francisco, Jossey-Bass, 1968.

Klein, S. M. 'Two systems of management: A comparison that produced organizational change', Sixteenth Annual Meeting, Industrial Relations Research Association, December 1963, 17–26.

Kluckhohn, C., and Murray, H. A. *Personality in nature, society and culture*, New York, Knopf, 1949.

Kluckman, C. 'Common humanity and diverse cultures'. In D. Lerner (ed.), *The human meaning of the social sciences*, Meridian Books, 1959, p. 253.

Kohn, M. L. *Class and conformity: A study of values*, Homewood, Ill., Dorsey Press, 1969.

Kohn, M. L., and Schooler, C. 'Class occupation and orientation', *American Sociological Review*, 1969, 34 (5), 659–758.

Kornhauser, A. W. *Mental health of the industrial worker*, New York, Wiley, 1965.

Lawrence, P. R., and Lorsch, J. W. *Organization and environment: Managing differentiation and integration*, Boston, Division of Research, Harvard University, Graduate School of Business Administration, 1967.

Lewin, K. *A dynamic theory of personality*, New York, McGraw-Hill, 1935.

Likert, R. *The human organization: Its management and values*, New York, McGraw-Hill, 1967.

New patterns of management, New York, McGraw-Hill, 1961.

Litwin, G. H., and Stringer, R., Jr. *Motivation and organizational climate*, Boston, Harvard University, Division of Research, Graduate School of Business Administration, 1968.

Lobb, J., and Ellis, C. D. 'Corporate surgery: How disinvestments can boost profits by cutting sales', *Corporate Finance*, 1970, 11 (3), 17–22.

Lorsch, J. W., and Lawrence, P. R. *Studies in organizational design*, Homewood, Ill., R. D. Irwin, 1970, pp. 16–35.

McClelland, D., *et al. The achievement motive*, New York, Appleton-Century-Crofts, 1953.

McGregor, D. *The human side of enterprise*, New York, McGraw-Hill, 1960.

Maddi, S. R. 'The pursuit of consistency and variety'. In R. P. Abelson, E. Aronson, W. J. McGuire, T. M. Newcombe, M. J. Rosenbert, and P. H. Tannenbaum (eds.), *Theories of cognitive consistency: A source-book*, Chicago, Rand McNally, 1968.

Mann, F., and Williams, L. R. 'Some effects of the changing work environment in the office', *Journal of Social Issues*, 1962, 18(3), 90–101.

Maslow, A. *Motivation and personality*, New York, Harper, 1954.

Meyer, H. 'Achievement motivation and industrial climates'. In R. Taguiri and G. H. Litwin (eds.), *Organizational climate*, Boston, Harvard University, Graduate School of Business Administration, 1968, 151–68.

Meyer, H., Kay, E., and French, J. 'Split roles in performance appraisal', *Harvard Business Review*, 1965, 43, 123–9.

Michael, D. *The unprepared society: Planning for a precarious future*, New York, Basic Books, 1968.

Miller, J. P. 'Social-psychological implications of Weber's model of bureaucracy: Relations among expertise, control, authority, and legitimacy', *Social Forces*, 1970, 49(1), 91–102.

Myers, M. S. 'Every employee a manager', *California Management Review*, 1968, 10(3).

Padfield, H. 'New industrial systems and cultural concepts of poverty', *Human Organization*, 1970, 29(1), 29–36.

Perlin, L. I. 'Alienation framework: A study of nursing personnel', *American Sociological Review*, 1962, 27(3), 314–35.

Perrow, C. 'Departmental power and perspectives in industrial firms'. In M. N. Zald (ed.), *Power in organizations*, Nashville, Tenn., Vanderbilt University Press, 1970*a*.

Organizational analysis: A sociological view, Belmont, Calif., Wadsworth Publishing Co., 1970*b*.

'A framework for the comparative analysis of organizations', *American Sociological Review*, 1967, 32(3), 194–208.

'Technology and organizational structure', *Proceedings of the 19th Annual Winter Meeting, Industrial Relations Research Association.*

Pugh, D. S. 'Modern organizational theory: A psychological and sociological study', *Psychological Bulletin*, 1966, 66(4), 235–51.

Pugh, D. S., Hickson, D. J., Hinings, C. R., and Turner, C. 'Dimensions of organizational structure', *Administrative Science Quarterly*, 1968, 13(1), 65–105.

Pugh, D. S., Hickson, D. J., Hinings, C. R., Macdonald, D. M., Turner, C., and Lupton, T. A. 'A conceptual scheme for organizational analyses', *Administrative Science Quarterly*, 1963, 8(3), 289–315.

Rackman, J., and Woodward, J. 'The measurement of technical variables'. In J. Woodward (ed.), *Industrial organization: Behavior and control*, New York, Oxford University Press, 1970.

Reedy, C. E. *The twilight of the presidency*, Cleveland, World Publishing, 1970.

Reeves, K. T., Turner, C., Barry, A., and Woodward, J. 'Technology and organizational behavior'. In J. Woodward (ed.), *Industrial organization: Behavior and control*, New York, Oxford University Press, 1970.

Reiss, A. J., Jr. 'Putting sociology into policy', *Social Problems*, 1970, 17(3), 289–94.

Sanford, N. 'The approach of the authoritarian personality'. In J. L. McCary (ed.), *The psychology of personality*, Plainfield, N.J., Logos, 1956.

Sayles, L. R. *Behavior in industrial work groups, prediction and control*, New York, Wiley, 1958.

Scanlon, J. M. 'Profit sharing under collective bargaining: Three case studies', *Industrial and Labor Relations Review*, 1948, 2(1), 58–75.

Shultz, G. P., and Cresara, R. P. 'Causes of industrial peace', The Lapointe Machine Tool Company and the U.S. Steelworkers of America, National Planning Association No. 10, November 1952.

'Worker participation on production problems', *Frontiers of Personnel Administration*, Department of Industrial Engineering, Columbia University, June 1951, 77–88.

Silverman, D. *The theory of organizations*, London, Heinemann, 1970.

Simon, H. A. *The science of the artificial*, Cambridge, Mass. M.I.T. Press, 1969.

Administrative behavior, New York, Glencoe Free Press, 1947.

Sirota, D. 'A study of work measurement', Sixteenth Annual Meeting, Industrial Relations Research Association, December 1963, 6–16.

Sloane, L. 'What happened behind the scenes as Ling was deposed', Financial Section of *New York Times*, 19 July 1970, p. 10.

Smelser, N. J., and Davis, J. A. *Sociology*, Englewood Cliffs, N.J., Prentice-Hall, 1969.

Sofer, C. *Men in mid-career*, New York, Cambridge University Press, 1970.

Stodgill, R., and Koehler, K. *Measures of leadership structure and organization change*, Columbus, Ohio, Personnel Research Board, Ohio State University, 1952.

Strauss, G. 'Organizational behavior and personnel relations'. Reprint 346, Institute of Industrial Relations, University of California, Berkeley, 1970.

'Some notes on power-equalization'. In H. J. Leavitt (ed.), *The social science of organizations: Four perspectives*, Englewood Cliffs, N.J., Prentice-Hall, 1963, pp. 34–84.

Street, D. *Inmate social organization: A comparative study of juvenile correctional institutions*, University of Michigan, Department of Sociology, 1962.

Street, D., Vinter, R., and Perrow, C. *Organization for treatment*, New York, The Free Press, 1966.

Tagiuri, R., and Litwin, G. H. (eds.), *Organizational climate*, Boston, Harvard University, Graduate School of Business, 1968.

Tannenbaum, A. *Control in organizations*, New York, McGraw-Hill, 1968.

Thompson, D. *Organizations in action*, New York, McGraw-Hill, 1967.

'The tales of three losers', *Time*, 27 July 1970, pp. 64–5.

Tornatzky, L. G., Fairweather, G. W., and O'Kelly, L. I. 'A Ph.D program aimed at survival', *American Psychologist*, 1970, 25(9), 884–8.

Trist, E., *et al. Organizational choice*, London, Tavistock Publications, 1962.

Vinter, R., and Janowitz, M. 'The comparative study of juvenile correctional institutions', a Research Report, University of Michigan, 1961.

Von Neumann, J. *The computer and the brain*, New Haven, Yale University Press, 1958.

Walker, C., and Guest, R. *The man on the assembly line*, Boston, Mass., Harvard University Press, 1952.

Webber, R. A. 'Perceptions of interactions between superiors and subordinates', *Human Relations*, 1970, 23(3), 235–48.

White, R. 'Motivation reconsidered: The concept of competence', *Psychological Review*, 1959, 66, 297–334.

Whyte, W. F. *Organizational behavior*, Homewood, Ill., R. D. Irwin, 1970.

Whyte, W. F., *et al. Money and motivation*, New York, Harper, 1955.

Whyte, W. F., and Hamilton, E. *Action research for management*, Homewood, Ill., Irwin-Dorsey, 1964.

Woodward, J. (ed.), *Industrial organization: Behavior and control*, New York, Oxford University Press, 1970.
Industrial organization: Theory and practice, New York, Oxford University Press, 1965.
Zupanov, J., and Tannenbaum, A. S. 'The distribution of control in some Yugoslav industrial organizations as perceived by members'. In A. S. Tannenbaum (ed.), *Control in organizations*, New York, McGraw-Hill, 1968.
Zurcher, L. A., Jr. *Poverty Warriers*, Austin, University of Texas Press, 1970.

INDEX